MURDER ON A LONELY ROAD

MURDER ON A LONELY ROAD

GEORGE PAWLACZYK
AND
BETH HUNDSDORFER

BERKLEY BOOKS, NEW YORK

THE BERKLEY PUBLISHING GROUP
Published by the Penguin Group
Penguin Group (USA) Inc.
375 Hudson Street, New York, New York 10014, USA
Penguin Group (Canada), 90 Eglinton Avenue East, Suite 700, Toronto, Ontario M4P 2Y3, Canada
(a division of Pearson Penguin Canada Inc.) • Penguin Books Ltd., 80 Strand, London WC2R 0RL,
England • Penguin Group Ireland, 25 St. Stephen's Green, Dublin 2, Ireland (a division of Penguin
Books Ltd.) • Penguin Group (Australia), 250 Camberwell Road, Camberwell, Victoria 3124, Australia
(a division of Pearson Australia Group Pty. Ltd.) • Penguin Books India Pvt. Ltd., 11 Community
Centre, Panchsheel Park, New Delhi—110 017, India • Penguin Group (NZ), 67 Apollo Drive,
Rosedale, Auckland 0632, New Zealand (a division of Pearson New Zealand Ltd.) • Penguin Books
(South Africa) (Pty.) Ltd., 24 Sturdee Avenue, Rosebank, Johannesburg 2196, South Africa

Penguin Books Ltd., Registered Offices: 80 Strand, London WC2R 0RL, England

The publisher does not have any control over and does not assume any responsibility
for author or third-party websites or their content.

MURDER ON A LONELY ROAD

A Berkley Book / published by arrangement with the author

PUBLISHING HISTORY
Berkley premium edition / September 2012

ISBN: 978-0-425-25034-1

BERKLEY®
Berkley Books are published by The Berkley Publishing Group,
a division of Penguin Group (USA) Inc.,
375 Hudson Street, New York, New York 10014.
BERKLEY® is a registered trademark of Penguin Group (USA) Inc.
The "B" design is a trademark of Penguin Group (USA) Inc.

PRINTED IN THE UNITED STATES OF AMERICA

10 9 8 7 6 5 4 3 2 1

Most Berkley Books are available at special quantity discounts for bulk purchases
for sales, promotions, premiums, fund-raising, or educational use. Special books, or
book excerpts, can also be created to fit specific needs.

For details, write: Special Markets, The Berkley Publishing Group,
375 Hudson Street, New York, New York 10014.

ACKNOWLEDGMENTS

Special thanks to University at Albany journalism professor Rosemary Armao for her day-to-day help with the writing, and to: Shannon Jamieson Vazquez, our editor at The Berkley Publishing Group in New York City; Claire Gerus, our agent, owner of the Claire Gerus Literary Agency in Tucson; and to our bosses at the *Belleville News-Democrat*, Gary Dotson, city editor, and Jeffry Couch, executive editor, for their support. And we are very grateful to former Christian County Sheriff Dwight McNiel and his wife, Marcella, for their invaluable assistance.

O villain, villain, smiling damned villain.

—HAMLET

CHAPTER 1

JUST JACKIE

The cowboy heard "Hey!" and spun around, but there was no chance to duck as a bucket of dirty mop water hit him in the face, cascaded down his chest, and flowed over his rodeo belt buckle, pooling in his shorts.

"What the hell?" he yelled, furious. And then, he saw her.

In the café doorway a few feet away stood Jackie Johns, holding an empty mop bucket in trembling hands. The cowboy stepped back, astounded. The nicest, friendliest waitress at the Nixa Sale Barn Café had just drenched him in foul water. And he knew he deserved it!

Jackie was smiling, but it wasn't the dazzling, sunny smile she had used since grade school to charm folks in town. This was a thin, determined victory smile, and there was no mistaking its message. Abashed and scowling, the cowboy left without another word.

For a moment, there was silence when Jackie stepped back into the café. Then a few of her regular customers erupted in laughter, and one old boy who drove a cattle hauler actually applauded. Here was a real scrapper of a waitress, by golly. She could have been fired for dumping water on a paying customer, but hey, she was like them. She wouldn't take any crap from anybody, and they respected her for it.

The regulars all knew that the cowboy had pursued her for weeks, hanging around, getting in her way. He'd continued to ask her out, not taking kindly to her polite but firm rejections. When she wasn't looking, he took his petty revenge by loosening the tops on the salt and pepper shakers, then slipping salt into the creamers and chuckling as her customers spit out their food and hollered, "Jackie!"

Yeah, the cowboy had thought it was all a big joke and he'd been making trouble just to get even. Now, the regulars figured he deserved what he got.

Meanwhile, Jackie seemed to savor all the drama. It was like when she and her best friend, twenty-year-old Lisa Fitzpatrick, would drive around in high school in Lisa's station wagon, nicknamed the "Sin Wagon," and boys in beat-up cars would give chase as Jackie would yell out, taunting them. Then Lisa would press the pedal to the floor and, with the boys on their tail, the girls would frantically escape into the driveway of Lisa's parents' house, where they would both run like crazy for the back door. When they dared look out a window, the boys would still be parked in front, which didn't really bother them. In fact, Jackie and Lisa would look at each other and burst into excited laughter.

That had been only two years ago.

Now it was 1985, and Jackie was out of high school and working two jobs. At nineteen Jackie was an attractive girl: a former prom queen, slender with dark brown hair that she always kept lacquered in place. She possessed a friendly directness that invited many of the café's patrons to open up, and they often found themselves telling her their problems and discussing personal issues usually kept private. Her dad teasingly called her "Ann Landers." Regulars would sit and chat as Jackie rolled silverware in napkins, swept the floors, or filled the salt and pepper shakers, and she'd smile as they talked on and on.

As for what Jackie was really like when she wasn't being all perky and cute, her boss, Jerry Estes, probably knew her as well as anyone. He often told friends she was like a daughter to him, as she'd worked at the café since she was fifteen years old.

The Sale Barn Café was a small restaurant just fifty or so yards off Highway 160 in Nixa. The diner-sized place was part of Jerry's much larger cattle operation, based in the auction barn behind the café. Cattlemen and their helpers turn their trucks off Highway 160 onto the narrow side road that runs beside the café to bring their stock to the huge auction barn filled with stalls for the steers. The barn was directly behind the café and down a small hill. On auction days the café would be jammed until perhaps an hour before the usual 10 P.M. closing time.

Jerry recalled that Jackie sometimes said and did zany things, like when she accidentally spilled coffee on a young man and then quickly rubbed at his lap with a towel, mindless of where her hand was reaching. The customer had been shocked at first, but then he laughed at the wide-eyed waitress, who blushed and apologized.

In early 1985, Jackie had decided to drop out of the small Missouri regional college near her home in Nixa that she had attended for only a few months. By the time the days got really hot in June, she was waitressing at the café and working full-time at the customer service desk at a local K-Mart.

Jackie was living with her parents in their trailer in Nixa, a Missouri village of less than two thousand residents. She had no set plans for the future, and when she felt like socializing, she'd meet others her age at the local 7-11 parking lot when they weren't working or at school.

Jackie had a boyfriend, twenty-three-year-old Cody Wright, and was even considering marrying him, but she wasn't really sure about tying herself down permanently. Like Jackie, he worked for Jerry Estes, but rather than waiting tables, Cody handled the chores associated with selling the big steers, animals that could weigh 1,200 pounds or more. He worked in the auction barn and sometimes even slept there in a bunkhouse if he finished late and was exhausted.

And then there was Jackie's cash flow problem. Although she worked two jobs, Jackie always seemed to be short of money. Once, she'd been so desperate, she'd even borrowed from her boss Jerry to pay for her books at college.

When she dropped out of school, her friends weren't too concerned. They knew Jackie would just plow straight ahead, cheerful, optimistic, and charmingly free-spirited.

Besides, Jackie was still Nixa's most popular young woman. She was known as the town's "It Girl." In high school, Jackie had been a homecoming and prom queen and a cheerleader. Then, a year after graduation, she'd won a local beauty contest. The improbably titled Nixa Sucker Day festival drew thousands each May from all over southwest Missouri. It was a crazy event: Buy a mug of beer and eat a fried filet of sucker, one of the lowliest of river fish. There was even sucker soup! The event featured rides and games and a street dance to entertain the celebrants.

When Jackie was crowned "Sucker Day Queen," she and her friend Lisa treated the whole thing as a joke. As friendly rivals for the title, the girls had told friends that if they voted for them and one of them won, they would dress up in homemade fish suits and parade up and down Main Street. When Jackie won and Lisa was the runner-up, they were thrilled—and then laughed as they told their friends to forget it, they weren't dressing up like fools in fish suits!

Old folks—that is, anyone much over thirty—still stopped Jackie when they saw her on the street to ask, "How are things going?" They told Jackie she was such a promising young woman and so polite; such a refreshing change from most young people. Yes, she was certainly on her way to a better life, they all agreed.

Jackie's answer was always the same. "Things are great, and thanks for asking!"

While she was freewheeling in many ways, she was obsessive about her looks, and her hair, in particular, had to be just so. In fact, she bought Aqua Net hair spray nearly as often as she bought cigarettes.

Her obsession with tidiness didn't extend to her beloved 1976 black Camaro. In fact, its red interior was so littered you couldn't see the floor mats. Still, it was a hot car, as the local teenage boys told her all the time.

Jackie just smiled and took it all in. Life was good.

But her closest friends knew there was another side to Jackie Johns. There were times when she shed her sweet, girl-next-door demeanor and let loose. She could smoke and drink with the best of them, and when she uttered an occasional obscenity, her friends would laugh because it seemed so out of place coming from her.

Jackie even had a stolen I.D. and liked to show it off. The I.D. allowed her to buy an occasional six-pack of beer at a store up in Springfield where people didn't know her. Other friends knew she had dated a married man who had a big job at a shopping mall, but that turned out to be just a brief fling.

Nixa's downtown consisted of only a few blocks. It had seemed like a big place when Jackie was growing up, but now that she was close to turning twenty, she confided to close friends that she wanted more than life in a small Missouri town. The problem was, she didn't know what she wanted, or how to get it.

She told a close friend that sometimes she dreamed of loading up the trunk of her Camaro with clothes and lots of cold beer and just driving, maybe to Arkansas or to Mexico. But her roots were strong, and held her there in Nixa.

On this night at the café, she had wielded a mop bucket like a magic wand. It had been so satisfying to douse that smug bastard, but afterward, Jackie couldn't stop shaking. She had been so scared and angry. She'd never done anything like that before—dumping water on a customer. What would Jerry say if he found out?

But when she calmed down, she said she felt so good she wanted to jump into her Camaro, turn the radio to blasting, and just drive. Anywhere.

CHAPTER 2

A FOGGY NIGHT

Jackie grabbed the ringing phone just as she arrived for work at the customer service desk at Springfield's K-Mart. "I like what you got on today," the male caller said. "You look really sexy."

She recognized the caller's voice but had no idea what his name was or what he looked like. She knew him only as the disembodied voice known as "The Jerk." That was what other young women in Jackie's circle of friends in the Nixa area called him. Jackie had talked to others who had gotten the calls. They had agreed that the caller sounded like a teenage boy around seventeen or eighteen years old, and his calls were always obscene.

"Know what I want to do to you?" he asked in a low voice.

Jackie laughed and teased, and a coworker had heard her say, "What? What do you want to do?" Then she

hung up before he could answer. The cops had been trying to catch the kid for months but had gotten nowhere.

But this time he had called just as she arrived for the
start of her night shift at K-Mart, and it was just getting
dark. Before, he had always called her home number at
her parents' mobile home in Nixa. Suddenly, she felt nervous. She knew there were pay phones in the parking lot
and boldly walked outside to see if she could spot the
caller if he was still around. She saw several cars pulling
out, and a teenage boy drove past in a minivan, looked at
Jackie, and smiled. So did the driver of a Firebird, who
looked to be in his twenties.

She walked to the first of the cart corrals and scanned
the parking lot. Then she realized it was pointless: Every
young guy who drove past would give her the once-over,
and how would she know if one of them was "The Jerk"?

Later, when she was in the women's wear section
checking a price for a blouse, Jackie felt as if she was
being watched. At first she didn't look up, and then she
heard her employee number announced on the public
address system. It meant the cashier out front was getting antsy and needed to know the price. She had to
hurry, but she didn't move. There was no doubt now—
she definitely felt someone's eyes on her.

She whirled around to see a boy of about twelve staring right at her. He held a skateboard and flushed, then
turned away and hurried off toward the toy section. "I'm
really getting freaked out," she told herself as she returned to the front of the store.

On a smoke break, Jackie confided to a female coworker

her odd feelings lately, like somebody was always watching her. She also told her about a disturbing phone call she had gotten a few weeks earlier on her bedroom telephone. Her friend Dayna (who also waitressed at the café) had been over, so Jackie asked her to answer.

Dayna picked it up and then made a face. It was that creepy guy, Gerry, a regular customer from the café, who had a voice much different than the teenage, whiny voice the young women described to police after they received a call from "The Jerk." The busy café attracted its share of flirtatious assholes, of course, like the cowboy Jackie had doused. Who among them could resist kidding around with a pretty girl? Jackie had learned to deal with the flirting, but there was one customer who sometimes showed up at the café and gave Jackie and the other young waitresses the creeps not by saying anything, but just by staring at them with his faint, mocking smile.

Gerry Carnahan was in his late twenties, not much older than Jackie, but he was married to an older woman and had a stepdaughter, Sara, who was nineteen, the same age as Jackie. Jackie didn't really know Gerry, but she had briefly worked at his father's factory in Nixa. The elder Carnahan was rumored to be the richest man in town.

For some reason, Gerry Carnahan always tried to sit in Jackie's section, and if there wasn't an empty table there, he'd act up and behave badly with the other waitresses. The women did their best to ignore him, but when they were forced to take his order, they made sure to call him "sir," making it clear that he wasn't one of

their favorites. The waitresses always called their preferred customers by their first names.

Jackie, usually unruffled, was disturbed when Gerry
called her at home. She had handed the phone to Dayna
and whispered that she should tell him she was busy.
Then she had gone over and checked outside her bedroom window. All she really knew about Gerry was that
his rich father, Garnett Carnahan, lived at the end of a
road named after his family, Carnahan Way. Dayna said
Jackie couldn't talk and hung up.

The elder Carnahan's house was only about a half mile
from the trailer owned by Jackie's parents, but she
couldn't actually see it from her bedroom window. However, the day the call came from Gerry, she quickly closed
the blinds on her bedroom window, and after that, she
kept them closed.

Lately, because she felt she was being watched, Jackie
would park near the store's entrance when she came to
work. She knew this was a rule violation, because K-Mart
employees were supposed to park near the back of the
lot, leaving the best spaces for paying customers. But
Jackie was uneasy about walking that far at night after
her shift ended. If the bosses wanted to fire her for it,
well, she could always find another job.

And then another guy from the café did the weirdest
thing. A few days after Valentine's Day, Jackie showed up
at 5 P.M. for her regular shift at the Sale Barn. To her
dismay, she found that this guy—whom everyone called
"Dub"—had left a single red rose and a big, expensive

heart-shaped box of chocolates in a paper bag with her name on it.

Folks at the café knew Jackie's boyfriend was Cody Wright. But insiders also knew that the relationship was getting tense lately because Cody had begun seeing his ex-wife again. Although the couple had been legally separated when Jackie and Cody first became an item, now, with this new development, Jackie wasn't sure where their relationship was going. But Cody would later sign a sworn statement to police that while he had met with his former wife, there was no romance going on.

So what was up with this "Dub" guy? He was clearly not in Jackie's league. In fact, nobody talked to him about much of anything, so he wasn't likely to know about Jackie's problems with Cody. He was also a bit slow-witted. He chewed tobacco and spit it out in a jar he kept in his jacket pocket, a practice that so grossed out some of the waitresses, they wouldn't serve him. But he had never been rude to any of the girls. And Jackie, of course, had been polite to him, even if his habits did make her skin crawl. Dub was just this big old guy who left nice tips for the waitresses—he was hardly considered dating material, being in his midforties and kind of scruffy looking.

And then, that day, there it was: a big paper bag with "For Jackie" scrawled on the outside. Some of the girls peeked inside, and Alice, the cook, a big smile on her face, said, "Why Jackie, you have a secret admirer."

Inside, Jackie found the rose, the heart-shaped box of chocolates, and a Valentine's Day card with a signature she didn't recognize. One of the regulars told her it was Dub's real name.

Jackie pitched the rose and after work made a beeline straight to Lisa's house, where they devoured the chocolates and laughed about Dub. It was mean, they knew, but they weren't really mean girls. They would never have laughed in his face. But Dub as a boyfriend? Come on!

"Give me a break!" Jackie had laughed.

And then a few days later, one of the café customers said that Dub had just been released from the Marian Center, a privately-operated mental hospital. That news necessitated another trip to Lisa's house, but this time Jackie was worried. Could she be in danger from a loony tunes guy?

However, Dub was never seen again, and word came a few weeks later from a long-haul trucker that he had been arrested down in Newton County. The trucker said he didn't know exactly what police had charged Dub with, but they thought he might have shot someone.

Throughout the first six months of 1985, Jackie spent a lot of time hanging out with Lisa and Dayna. It seemed as if they were always together, although Lisa tended to avoid the Sale Barn Café. The cattle auctions that Jerry Estes held in the big barn out back just weren't her thing.

It was the same with Jackie. The café was one thing, but she never walked along the path leading down the small hill to the auction barn. And she refused to go near the cattle.

Dayna, who worked part-time for the on-call vet in a

small office at the back of the auction barn as well as waitressing, thought Jackie's reluctance had something to do with the visiting veterinarian who occasionally had to lethally inject an animal because of an injury suffered during shipping. Jackie avoided anything to do with animals suffering and was nervous about being near the rambling auction barn, especially at night when the stalls were empty and the low-lying barn in back of the café was often shrouded in fog.

Dayna was an animal lover, too, just like Jackie and Lisa, but she had the mental toughness to do what was necessary when an animal was hurt. She actually wanted to be a cop, and had already enrolled at the local police academy, where she attended classes.

Jackie had tons of friends and was rarely alone. When she wasn't with Dayna or Lisa, she was at the parking lot of the 7-11 on Highway 160 just outside Nixa. It had a pay phone in the parking lot and was convenient in case she needed cigarettes or Aqua Net.

But on a chilly, rainy night in May, just before midnight, Jackie found herself alone in the 7-11 parking lot. When forty-one-year-old Jewell Glotta pulled in at the convenience store just outside Nixa on her way to work near midnight, she saw what appeared to be a distraught teenage girl sitting coatless on a cement curb with the rain dripping off her hair and mascara running down her cheeks. The girl sat beside a black Camaro and was leaning her head against the driver's door and weeping.

Glotta had no idea that this girl was Nixa's own "It

Girl"—the promising, desirable Jackie Johns, the girl with the golden future.

Then she realized she had seen her before. It had been a week earlier in the same parking lot around the same time near midnight. This same girl with the same car was then twenty cents short of paying for two dollars' worth of gas, and Glotta had been happy to loan her the twenty cents. And when she again ran into her a few days later inside the 7-11, Jackie had repaid her the money.

But what was this? Why was Jackie crying in the rain?

"Are you all right? Are you sick?" Glotta asked her. Jackie shook her head, but Glotta didn't know what that meant. She didn't think Jackie had been drinking; at least she didn't smell any alcohol when she sat next to her. But Jackie kept right on crying. And then a pay phone behind them began ringing. Jackie jumped up, grabbed the receiver, and screamed, "You dumb mother-fucker!"

Glotta was so surprised, she rushed into the 7-11, bought her snacks for work, and left. She never saw Jackie again.

Whatever that disturbing phone call in the rain had meant, Jackie never talked about it with Lisa or Dayna. Maybe it was about Cody. But by the time the hot weather arrived in the middle of June, he and Jackie had patched things up. He had given her forty dollars and a beautiful card on her birthday, and she'd put the card in her Camaro on a little shelf under the dashboard. She had turned twenty a week earlier on June 7.

On Saturday, June 15, 1985, Jackie was happily anticipating a day off work with friends. They planned to spend the day at nearby Table Rock Lake, where Lisa's parents owned a cabin on the water.

But once she was at the cabin, Jackie seemed unusually quiet.

Lisa and her boyfriend, Tony Ledford, and another couple were already at the cabin before Jackie and Cody showed up. They all drank piña coladas and then went down to the water. Lisa's family had bought her one of the first Jet Skis ever seen on the big lake, and she loved to gun it until the craft leaped over the waves.

Now, she circled just off the narrow beach, and Jackie begged her to be able to try it, but Lisa wouldn't let her. For some reason, Lisa just didn't want to share it that day. Later, she couldn't understand why she had been so mean to her best friend. It might have been something about the way Jackie was acting. She seemed bothered about something but hadn't talked her head off as usual. Lisa wondered whether they might be growing apart.

As the hot afternoon wore on, Jackie and Cody eventually gathered their towels and street clothes and, without a word, trudged up the embankment to the parking lot. They left without saying good-bye, strange behavior for the usually gregarious Jackie.

The next day, Sunday, Jackie called in sick to K-Mart. That, too, was unusual, as she rarely took time off.

The following morning, Monday, June 17, 1985, Jackie got out of bed early for her morning shift at the café. She gazed into the bathroom mirror and, using a rattail comb, teased her bangs and put on her lip gloss and blush. Then she sprayed a fog of Aqua Net around her. Jackie refused to be seen in public unless her hair and makeup were just right, no matter how long it took.

After the breakfast rush at work, she left to have Sonya, one of the waitresses from the café, cut her hair. She told Sonya it was time for change in her life, and a new hairstyle would be the first step.

An hour later, at 3:15 P.M., Jackie walked through the door of the Tanning Saloon, where she also worked a couple of hours a week in exchange for free time under the lamps.

"How do you like my haircut?" Jackie asked Cindy, the owner, and then, instead of waiting for her answer, she headed straight for a tanning bed. Cindy Hood knew something was wrong. Jackie always became the center of attention when she came into the salon, and she'd always have a joke, a bit of gossip, or a story. And she'd just had her hair cut—and everyone knew Jackie's hair was her obsession. So it was inconceivable that she didn't want to talk about it.

Hood thought about asking Jackie if there was something she could do to help whatever was bothering her, but then thought better of it. Later, she wished she had gone with her instincts.

About an hour later, twenty-two-year-old Wanda Smith showed up at the tanning salon. She, too, noticed that Jackie was uncharacteristically quiet.

"What's wrong?" Wanda asked her.

"I don't want to talk about it," Jackie said. "I can't talk about it."

"Talk about what?" said Wanda.

"Oh, just nothing. Nothing. I gotta go." Jackie hastily stepped out the front door and then walked to her Camaro. The women in the salon watched Jackie walk to her car, then saw her do an odd thing: Jackie pulled the driver's seat forward before she got in and looked in the back, as if checking to see if anyone was hiding in the rear of the car.

Then, she drove straight to her parents' home and changed out of her shorts and T-shirt into a blouse and jeans. She was due back at the café at 5 P.M.

At around 8 P.M. Lisa got a phone call. It was Jackie calling during her break at the café. "I gotta talk to you tonight. Meet me after work," Jackie said.

"I can't go out tonight," Lisa told her. "My mother won't let me—it's too foggy to drive."

"But you gotta," Jackie said. "I gotta talk to you about something. I can't talk on the phone. It's important."

Lisa told Jackie to wait and then set the receiver down. She asked her mother if she could go out, but her mother wouldn't budge. Lisa would never forget what her mother said.

"You're not going out. It's foggy enough for murder."

That night, Jackie wore a red and white striped blouse. Alice, the cook, remembered the blouse because Jackie had traded clothes with a girlfriend from Ozark, and the blouse was part of the exchange. She had been happy to get it.

Her coworkers remembered that Jackie's shift had been unremarkable except for when Cody's friend, Kirk Dooms, showed up. He had come to ask for Jackie's advice about his relationship with his girlfriend. Nixa's "Ann Landers" was on duty once again.

Alice saw them sitting on opposite sides of a booth. Jackie was leaning in, listening intently as Kirk discussed his romantic turmoil. Alice remembered that they talked for a half hour and then Dooms left.

Other employees would recall that at roughly 10:00 P.M., Jackie shook out the rugs and swept the floor. When she was finished cleaning, she met Cody in the parking lot, and he kissed her good night. Cody, who worked the cattle auction that night, was exhausted and told Jackie he was going straight home.

Jackie seemed happy as she said good night to Cody and drove off in her Camaro into the dense fog. Other waitresses and men from the auction would recall that she turned right on Highway 160, in the direction of the 7-11.

But something very unusual had happened about a half hour before the café closed at 10 P.M. Jackie had told Alice that she was going down to the auction barn, and later a hired hand, who didn't know Jackie, said he thought he saw a girl in a red and white striped blouse walking down the path to the auction barn.

The young man thought this was odd because there was no one down in the empty barns. The stalls were dark and smelled of cattle. The auction staff had left and buyers were on the road, hauling stock. The vet had closed his office and Dayna wasn't around. But the hired hand was sure he saw the girl walk all the way down the path and disappear into the first of the barns.

The next day, when Dayna learned about Jackie's trip to the auction barn, she was puzzled because Jackie had always been afraid to go down there. Why would she go there that particular night? Had Jackie been looking for her? What did she want?

Unfortunately, Dayna would never find out.

CHAPTER 3

BLOODY MONDAY

Jerry Estes sat straight up and swung his legs off the couch. He'd decided to stay the night at his office at the Sale Barn, and he'd slept deeply after a long day and night running his café and his cattle auction followed by an hour drinking beer with the cattle workers on the back of a flatbed truck in the parking lot.

He heard a pounding coming from the next room. Someone was at his office door. The pounding got louder, like a process server or a cop with a warrant. He pulled on jeans and a T-shirt but didn't turn on the light.

It was Alice, his cook, at the door. She usually showed up right around 5 A.M. on weekdays, often with Dayna, to get the café's fryers started. Now, Alice was so excited she was talking too fast for Jerry to understand. Dayna stood right behind her, looking extremely upset.

"Slow down! Slow down!" Jerry told Alice. "Start again."

It had something to do with his waitress Jackie Johns and her car, her precious Camaro. Nobody was inside, and it was sitting abandoned on the highway. The milk-man had spotted it, too.

Now, Alice took a deep breath, her eyes wide with fear for her friend.

"Easy, honey," Jerry said, waiting until she could speak. He didn't dare think about what all this could mean.

"It's Jackie's car," Alice said. "It's out on the road with the door open and I didn't see Jackie anywhere. You'd better not wait, Jerry. You'd better go. Maybe she's hurt or something!"

A heavy fog still lingered that morning, but Jerry sped along Highway 160, deserted at this early hour. In a few minutes, he arrived at the spot Alice had described, about two miles from the auction barn. A Camaro was parked on the shoulder of the road headed northbound toward Springfield amid signs of construction all around.

Jerry parked his pickup ten feet behind the black Chevy and immediately recognized it as Jackie's car, with its personalized license plate: "Jacki-1."

His pickup's headlights lit the scene, and, just as Alice had reported, the Camaro's driver's door was ajar. Jerry cautiously walked around the car and then came back to the driver's side, careful not to smudge any fingerprints, and pulled the door open.

When he looked inside, he felt his stomach churn. The car was a holy mess!

Jackie's open purse lay on the front floorboard, and he could see money inside it. The keys were in the ignition. Items of makeup were scattered about and the ashtray had been pulled out. It, too, lay on the floor.

But it was the sight of blood everywhere inside the car, mostly in the backseat, mixed in places with long strands of dark hair, that made him gasp. He instinctively stepped back as he struggled to absorb what he was seeing, and then quickly looked over the Camaro's roof to the field beyond, but no one was in sight.

The sun was just coming up, with the fields still in shadows. Not one car passed as Jerry forced down his rising gorge and took another look inside the Camaro. There was just enough light to see blood on the front seat on both the driver's and the passenger's sides. There were even splotches of blood along the top of the passenger's window.

And the backseat was far worse. With growing horror, Jerry realized that the big splotches of dark stain across the red cloth interior were blood mixed with what looked like dried leaves and dirt. On the floor in back, he saw bloody blue jeans with the legs rolled up and what appeared to be panties caught up in one of them.

He also spotted a blood-smeared bra.

That was enough. Jerry ran to his pickup to get back to the café, where he called the dispatcher at the Christian County Sheriff's Office in Ozark. The woman promised that she'd send help, and then Jerry shakily drove back to the Camaro to wait for the police.

Missouri State Highway Patrol trooper Billy Chadwick was the first to show up, with Sheriff Dwight McNiel right behind him. Then, a few minutes later, Sergeant Tom Martin from the Highway Patrol pulled up. The three police cruisers kept their emergency lights flashing as commuters to Springfield began passing the scene and word spread that something was up on Highway 160.

Jerry watched, his stomach in knots, as Chadwick and McNiel shone their flashlights into the Camaro's interior. Then they turned to him. "What happened here?" Chadwick asked.

Jerry told them that Alice, his cook, had said she'd seen the car at 5 A.M. when she came to work, and she'd awakened him to come take a look. She was worried, and now so was he—in fact, panicked was probably a more accurate word for how he felt.

He told the police that after arriving and seeing the blood, he had driven back to the office to call the sheriff's dispatcher, and had then returned immediately to the Camaro.

The four of them stood there. They all knew what had to happen next, but no one wanted to be the one to do it.

Someone had to open the trunk.

Finally, with a sense of dread, McNiel removed the keys from the Camaro's ignition and Chadwick trained his flashlight on the rear of the car. It was then, under the powerful beam, that Jerry noticed a faint, whitish dusting that seemed to encase the entire car, as if it had been driven across dirt roads at high speed. However, it looked like someone had wiped the dust away from a bread box–sized portion of the trunk lid, just above the lock.

Now, Jerry, Chadwick, and Martin watched intently as Sheriff McNiel inserted the key and the trunk popped open. The four men looked down into the dark trunk as Chadwick's beam illuminated the darkened interior. There was no body; only a spare tire, a tire iron, and scattered items of clothing.

Dwight McNiel was the first to break the silence. He murmured, "What have we here?" Using a stick from the road, he lifted an old-style bumper jack from between the spare tire and the rear wall of the trunk. It hadn't been immediately visible, but now Chadwick trained his light on the heavy, three-foot-long jack, as did McNiel, who held his flashlight with his free hand.

Jerry could not turn away, although he desperately wanted to. He knew what he was looking at. He had spent hundreds of hours working with cattle, including dealing with the bloody mess of the horn-shaving process. To handle steers safely, big shears are used to cut off the animals' horns. He knew the sight of smeared blood. And now, on the bumper jack, it seemed certain he was seeing the same gory stains he had come to know so well.

McNiel thought he saw hair on the lip of the jack, the part where the metal hook that goes under the edge of a car's bumper or frame is attached. "Is that blood there, too?" he asked Jerry.

"That's blood all right, all up and down that whole thing," Jerry said.

"It's everywhere! Jesus!"

The last thing Jerry ever thought he would be doing was staring at what had to be Jackie Johns's blood smeared all over an ordinary car bumper jack that had probably been used to kill her. It had to be her blood; who else would be in her car? She never let anyone drive it. And those long, dark hairs. They had to be Jackie's . . .

Dwight lowered the grisly jack and closed the trunk. Jerry knew he had to go straight back to the office because Dayna and Alice would be frantic and were waiting for his report.

And all he could tell them was what they already knew—that something terrible had happened to Jackie.

CHAPTER 4

--- --- --- --- ---

WHERE'S JACKIE?

At age thirty-two, Dwight McNiel was the youngest sheriff ever elected in Christian County, as far as folks could remember. On June 18, 1985, when he assumed shared command with the Springfield Police Department of the Jackie Johns missing person case, he had only been in office for five and a half months.

His temporary command post was the section of road outside Nixa heading north where highway cones surrounded Jackie's car. From the highway, he radioed Troop D of the Missouri State Highway Patrol in Springfield to alert them to what had been found. He was assisted by Highway Patrol sergeant Tom Martin, who had showed up at the Camaro just after McNiel.

Martin was head of the troop's Division of Drug and Crime Control, a fancy name for the state cops who investigated the swarms of meth dealers who were killing one another on back roads all over Christian and Taney counties. They also investigated any major crimes, and this was definitely shaping up to being one of them.

Tall and lanky, forty-four-year-old Martin had worn a badge for more than twenty years and was known to be a good listener. So good, in fact, that some folks thought he was taciturn. But that wasn't true; he just knew when to talk and when to listen. And he had an unnerving habit of waiting until a suspect had talked himself out, and then unerringly picked out the suspect's lies and contradictions like he was gathering apples that had fallen from a tree.

Sergeant Martin also had a way of bearing down and looking a suspect in the eye with unblinking intensity. It led some lawbreakers to believe that Martin wouldn't believe them even if they said the sky was blue on a cloudless day.

McNiel had served as chief deputy for the previous sheriff, Buff Lamb. He had worked many cases with Martin and the two had become friends. Now, as police photographers recorded the scene, McNiel and Martin decided it would be best to search the Camaro more thoroughly after it was safely stored in a garage. McNiel had the Camaro towed to a Chevrolet dealership's garage about six miles away in Ozark and just a few blocks from his office in the Christian County courthouse.

On the way to Ozark, with Martin following, McNiel used his radio to launch a search for Jackie. By that afternoon, hundreds of searchers who had heard from TV news reports or word of mouth that Jackie was missing showed up to volunteer at the sheriff's office in Ozark. From there, they left to scour fields and brush and the shoreline of Lake Springfield several miles north of where the Camaro had been found.

They searched on horseback, with ATVs, and on foot. Jerry Estes led a team of searchers mounted on horseback. Two helicopters and a half dozen private aircraft scanned the terrain.

Meanwhile, at the Chevy garage, McNiel handed Martin a pair of latex gloves and the two trained a set of bright lights into the Camaro's interior, keeping both doors wide open. McNiel and Martin intended to collect only what was obvious—the bloody jeans with the panties rolled up in one leg, the bloody bra, any obvious hairs, a blood sample, and Jackie's red and white striped blouse.

They carefully removed some of the leaves and soil with tweezers and a small scoop, working slowly and methodically. A deputy took photos as they went along. The team was careful not to erase or destroy any part of whatever story the Camaro's interior might reveal. Finally, after two hours, the car was towed to the Highway Patrol lab in Springfield for further examination.

The next morning both men, who had slept only a few hours, joined the search for Jackie. Martin rode the highways, looking for dirt roads that might reveal that whitish dust they had noticed on Jackie's car. Meanwhile, McNiel headed for the small airfield known grandly as "The Christian County Airport," where he kept a small plane.

If this were any other day, McNiel's spirits would have soared when he pulled up to his vintage 1946 Funk 885 C, painted a jaunty yellow with dark blue trim. It was the kind of airplane that the Allies had used to spot German tanks and infantry in Europe during World War II. McNiel had bought it from a county judge who'd found piloting the little plane too tricky.

But this was no time for nostalgia. It was the second day in the search for Jackie Johns, and everyone's face reflected grim determination. Jackie was a local girl, loved by everyone, and the task ahead was one they all loathed—searching for, and possibly finding, her body.

McNiel's deputy, Dale Reynolds, now joined his chief as both men put their shoulders to the tail section of the plane and pushed it ahead a few yards to the edge of the dirt runway. Then, McNiel strapped himself into the pilot seat and hit the ignition button as Reynolds climbed into the single passenger seat. He'd brought binoculars and a topographic map that included Lake Springfield. Neither man spoke as the small aircraft bounced and took off.

At five hundred feet, McNiel leveled off and turned northwest for the lake. They passed over hundreds of volunteers who waved from ATVs and horseback. The sheriff was grateful that he could quickly muster an army of searchers willing to tramp about on a brutally hot June day. That was because most of them knew and loved Jackie.

Once over the lake, McNiel dipped the Funk down to two hundred feet, a technical violation of local flight rules that he was going to ignore, given the extraordinary circumstances. Below them, boys on summer vacation dog-paddled along the reedy shoreline. Reynolds, who was training his binoculars on the lake, spotted the kids but paid little attention to them. McNiel was focused on the area over the plane's nose, dreading the hour that he feared was close by when a body would be found and he would have to tell his friends, Les and Shirley Johns, that their daughter was never coming home.

Four days after the discovery of Jackie's car, Sergeant Tom Martin eased into the middle seat of a canoe steadied by his friend, Sheriff Dwight McNiel. In the bow, a Greene County deputy held a paddle at the ready as a conservation officer got in and took the remaining seat.

A surreal scene was developing at the boat-launching ramp on the shore close to the southern end of Lake Springfield. A crowd of onlookers had already gathered, drawn by the presence of dozens of police cars. Martin turned and scanned the water. His job as supervisor of the area's primary Highway Patrol crime investigation unit had called him to hundreds of places where a dead body was to be expected: mangled car wrecks, remote farm fields, barrooms streaked with blood. But this time was different, unlike anything he had experienced in his twenty-plus years of law enforcement. The body of Jackie Johns, the focus of a four-day manhunt, the largest in the history of all of southwestern Missouri, could possibly be less than two hundred feet away. That's where earlier that morning fishermen said they had spotted a woman's naked body floating in the weeds. They claimed to have seen a body less than seventy-five yards from the shore in only a few feet of water. Martin knew they could be mistaken; he'd seen it happen before, as debris could easily take the form of human remains to an untried eye, especially in water.

If it was Jackie, her remains were about to be recovered in full view of a throng of onlookers, including news teams from three television stations.

Martin hated this scenario, preferring to handle such delicate police work without zoom lens–equipped television cameras a few yards away.

It would only take seconds to guide the canoe to the spot about two hundred feet away where Martin could just make out something whitish on the surface. As they rowed toward the area, his mind raced.

Everything within him hoped the body wasn't Jackie's, but he knew the odds were against him. The condition of the Camaro made finding her alive seem hopeless—there was just so much blood . . . and that bloody car jack.

Years later, he would remember in detail what he had been thinking as he rode in the canoe. He knew what they were going to find and he damn well didn't want to find it. He had investigated at least two hundred homicides, and he'd seen just about every form of death, including that of innocent children. Somehow, he'd managed to compartmentalize the faces of dead children, or women, or sometimes men, but he hadn't forgotten them. He said he sometimes dreamed about them, but kept tight control of his emotions.

This case was a real test, however. Maybe it was all the talk about "Jackie the beauty queen," the town's darling. But Martin would recall that it was more than that. Jackie Johns was the same age as his only child, his daughter, Debbie, an age when she'd been on the verge of becoming something, maybe following a dream.

Now, it looked as if he would find out in just a few seconds whether Jackie Johns would ever have a chance to realize her dreams.

The canoe glided toward whatever it was that lay trapped in the weeds, and again, Martin's thoughts turned to Debbie; he would later recount when asked about that awful day. He worried about her. Had he been spending enough time with his daughter? His job as commander of an undermanned Highway Patrol crime unit kept him away from home until late in the evening, unless he was on a stakeout. And then he might be gone for days. He now promised himself that he would find more time for Debbie, whatever it took.

Maybe it was just an instinctive reaction, something any father might feel when it seemed that someone else's kid had come to a horrific end, and maybe it was reflex. When facing the unthinkable, you tend to think of your loved ones.

Martin didn't know what Jackie dreamed she would someday become. But what he had learned about her during those four days assured him that she hadn't run away or been involved in criminal activities.

Martin's long experience as a homicide investigator told him that young women from good homes who disappeared under highly suspect circumstances usually ended up badly. It was just the plain truth. Hundreds of thick brown investigative folders back at Troop D Headquarters in Springfield described such scenarios in excruciating detail.

The deputy gently paddled while the state conservation officer guided the craft at the rear until they arrived at the spot. They immediately saw that what the fishermen had spotted wasn't debris. It was indeed the nude body of a woman with dark hair, floating facedown. With a gloved hand, Martin gently grasped an arm, but didn't turn her over. They led the body slowly along until they reached the edge of the boat ramp where Springfield detectives were waiting with a clean white sheet.

The sheet was placed under the remains and then lifted onto the ramp. The crowd watched silently, and TV cameramen stayed behind the yellow crime scene tape, while training their powerful telephoto lenses on the incredible scene unfolding in front of them.

When the body was turned over, Martin knew immediately that this was Jackie. The water in the lake had been unusually cool, and the body was well preserved, making her easily recognizable from the Johns family photographs he had in his police cruiser.

"Damn!" he murmured as he noted the bloody gaping hole in Jackie's right temple, as if she had been struck with a heavy object, and he immediately recalled the bloody jack from the Camaro's trunk. It certainly could have been the murder weapon.

On her left hand, he saw two inexpensive rings that had been described by Jackie's mom, Shirley. One was a silver ring with a green stone and another looked like an opal.

Martin stepped carefully out of the canoe and felt his face grow hot as the anger he had learned to carefully control now welled up. Clenching his fists, he watched as Jackie's remains were put in a body bag and placed into an ambulance.

A selfish, brutal coward had taken Jackie from her family and then, when he was finished with her, had dropped her in the lake like trash. There had to be a special place in hell for someone who would do such a thing. Many years later, Martin said that as he watched Jackie's body placed into an ambulance to be taken to the police morgue in Springfield, he steeled himself for the job ahead: finding the monster who had done this to one of Nixa's own.

And there was no way on earth that Jackie's murderer was going to remain at large if Sergeant Tom Martin had anything to say about it.

CHAPTER 5

A FUNERAL

Sheriff Dwight McNiel checked his watch. It was nearly 10:30 A.M. on Saturday, June 22. He parked in the Johns driveway beside their Ford pickup, and then sat there, gathering his thoughts and emotions, girding himself for the painful task that lay just moments away.

For a long moment, he didn't move. Then he saw the rear door of the mobile home swing open and Shirley Johns appeared in the doorway, arms helplessly at her sides. He had known her since he was a teenager, and now, she looked directly at him, and he couldn't turn away. Would she forgive him for what he had to tell her? Would she ever again allow him into her home for coffee and conversation with the painful memory of his words forever in her heart?

Only an hour earlier, her daughter's remains had been found out at the lake, and he had watched helplessly as

Jackie's body was wrapped in a sheet. By late that afternoon, it would be flown 150 miles to Columbia, Missouri, where an autopsy would be performed. McNiel would travel in a Cessna to fly to the autopsy and act as the legally required official witness. It was out of the question that McNiel would send someone in his place.

Finally, he opened his squad car door, took a deep breath, and slowly got out of the car. He walked toward Les and Shirley, unable to keep the worst possible news from showing on his face. But Shirley was already weeping. She knew.

When Jackie Johns went missing, for many in her hometown it felt as if Dorothy had been whisked off to an evil land of Oz. It was especially hard for Dwight McNiel, who remembered when Jackie still played with dolls. Her disappearance brought trouble to his own doorstep as well.

Now, he had to push aside his sorrow and find out all he could about Jackie's last days, good, bad, or indifferent. If he had any hope of catching her killer, they had to act quickly; most murders are usually solved within forty-eight hours if at all. Right now, he needed to single out and then interview the key people among Jackie's friends and acquaintances, especially any enemies.

For the time being he had already obtained some information from a few of Jackie's close friends and coworkers at the Sale Barn. Mostly it was basic, fun-loving stuff that hinted at Jackie's independent, mildly rebellious side. But what twenty-year-old woman didn't want to live it up a little?

McNiel learned that Jackie Johns had been nineteen years old when she got her dream car, the 1976 Camaro hardtop. The payments were fifty-four dollars a month, and she turned that car into her private world; a safe place where she could drop her "everybody's sweetheart" role and smoke and drink beer bought by older friends or by herself with an I.D. that said she was twenty-one. She kept extra sets of clothes, a hairbrush, lipstick, and mascara in the trunk in case she required a quick change in hair, makeup, and wardrobe. The Camaro also came with a cassette player, which was a big deal in 1985.

At home in Nixa, Jackie would drive her car with the windows rolled down, radio blaring, and the townsfolk staring and sometimes shaking their heads. They knew that even a town sweetheart wasn't always perfect.

And now, those days were all over.

As McNiel delivered the news to Les and Shirley that their daughter's body had been found, the couple collapsed upon each other.

There would never be a wedding or a college graduation. Shirley would never hug Jackie's children, and Les wouldn't get to take Jackie's sons or daughters fishing. But most upsetting to the couple was the fact that Jackie would never get the chance to live a long, happy life with those who loved her. And there were Jackie's three older sisters, Joyce, Janis, and Jeanne. They had lost their baby sister.

"I'm sorry to have to do this now," Dwight McNiel, now in his official role of sheriff, told Shirley and Les, "but I've got to ask you some questions about Jackie. They just can't wait."

At first, he just let Shirley talk, and doing so seemed to bring some life back into her.

She admitted she'd been disappointed that Jackie had dropped out of college, but her daughter had worked two jobs and bought her car with her own money, even if sometimes she lagged a bit on a payment.

But while she admired her daughter's ambitious nature, Shirley had always felt uneasy about Jackie's waitressing job at the Sale Barn Café. She believed it attracted rough customers, guys who made a living buying and selling cattle and horses. These were tough men involved in tough business; raising cattle and trying to get the top price for their steers at Jerry Estes' auction in the big sale barn in back of the café.

"Mom, please don't worry. They don't mean any harm," Jackie had told her again and again. "I can take care of myself." And most of the time, she could.

But men trooped in nearly nonstop at the popular café, and Jackie worked long hours, hauling plates to and from the kitchen. The men were loud and loved to kid around with the waitresses, and while some occasionally made off-color comments or indecent propositions, they quickly learned Jackie wouldn't put up with it.

She delivered comebacks and retorts that shut down the nonsense, and then she'd smile and take the order, deliver the plates, and pour a coffee heat-up.

After interviewing the distraught couple for an hour or so, McNiel left Shirley and Les Johns to plan their daughter's funeral. McNiel knew he had to assign plainclothes cops to the wake and funeral to watch for any suspicious-looking mourners. He also learned from the local funeral director that the funeral home couldn't accommodate the anticipated crowds of mourners, so the school superintendent had agreed to allow the funeral to be held in the high school gym.

The day of the services, at least a hundred floral arrangements were displayed around Jackie's coffin, and dozens of photographs of Jackie were shown in the school's lobby. As people poured in for the services, undercover officers discreetly snapped pictures of the crowd, just in case a suspect might show up.

Jackie's parents, Shirley and Les, and sisters Jeanne, Janis, and Joyce stood together near the casket. Les, tall and reserved in a dark suit, solemnly shook hands with the men and politely embraced the grief-stricken women, but Shirley's expression was closed and inscrutable.

Jackie's best friend, Lisa, just couldn't bring herself to come to the funeral and had stayed secluded at her parents' house for days after Jackie had gone missing. Jackie had been her best buddy, confidante, social manager, and hairdresser. It seemed impossible that she would never again pull up in that Camaro and blow the horn, yelling, "Come on! I'm waiting!"

Now, Lisa sat in her bedroom looking out a screened window at the tree-lined street. She remembered all the times she and Jackie had run errands together, picked out clothes together, shared secrets, put on makeup. And then there was "the ritual of the hair spray." At times, Lisa had been terrified that a spark would ignite the cloud of Aqua Net required for a Jackie hair intervention, blowing both of them to kingdom come!

And there was another fear that felt as if it would live within her for the rest of her life. Something had changed. Nixa had never been a totally innocent small town, and their lives hadn't been perfect. But the girls had never feared for their lives, and the possibility that Lisa might even know the person who had taken her friend's life shook her to her core.

On the day of Jackie's funeral, Lisa was in her bedroom, where she'd always felt safest, but the view through her curtained windows no longer soothed her. Her best friend was being buried today, and nothing would ever be the same.

―――――――

Before Jackie's murder, Dayna, who was attending the police academy, had lived alone in a trailer owned by her family. After the murder, her parents insisted she move home. They only relented and allowed her to move back to the trailer after they bought her a Rossi .38 revolver, which she kept in a drawer by her bed.

Dayna didn't feel scared so much as angry. After Jackie's body was found, Dayna bitterly wished her friend had had a gun with her the night she'd been murdered.

The day of Jackie's funeral, Dayna went home to change and noticed a pair of shoes she'd bought with Jackie. The two friends had bought matching pairs, white with the sides cut out, and the price tags were still attached. Dayna, who prided herself on keeping her cool, suddenly broke down and let herself feel the pain of her friend's loss.

A local clergyman had been asked to deliver the eulogy at Jackie's funeral. He checked with Shirley and Les to see what he should include, and they asked him to mention that Jackie worked hard, and that she always had a smile for everyone.

He knew it would be a challenge to make his eulogy live up to what the town expected to hear.

In the packed school gymnasium, hundreds of people tearfully listened to the town's farewell to their favorite daughter, friend, beauty queen . . . and waitress.

One of the girls stayed behind and waited for the crowd to thin out. Then, she asked a funeral associate to lift the lid of Jackie's coffin. She wanted to tuck a memento into the white satin lining enclosing the remains of Nixa's former homecoming queen.

It was a fresh can of Aqua Net hair spray.

CHAPTER 6

ATTITUDE

Less than twenty-four hours after Jackie Johns's body was pulled from Lake Springfield, Sheriff Dwight McNiel began to notice a stirring in the close-knit Nixa community. It started with Shirley and Les Johns, but that was to be expected. They had just lost their youngest child and wanted her killer caught, immediately.

If Shirley and Les were unrealistic and overly demanding, it was quickly forgiven. But to his surprise, friends that McNiel had known since he was a child began to stop him on the street and demand to know what he was doing about Jackie's murder. They became angry when he told them he couldn't share details of such an intense ongoing investigation, so he would turn away. In truth, he was unsure if silence was the right tactic, but he felt he had no choice.

This wasn't his first homicide, although it was the first

since he'd taken office nearly six months earlier, except for a murder/suicide. As a deputy and later as chief deputy, he had handled dozens of killings, but none came close to producing the public outcry for vengeance that hung over Nixa and Christian County after Jackie Johns's body was found. Her murder dominated the front page and television newscasts.

On some nights, entire radio talk shows were dedicated to discussing her murder. Reporters called him on the hour, and some even staked out the sheriff's office. Others tried to tail him. McNiel was shocked; he'd never expected this reaction.

But most of all, what McNiel couldn't get used to were the stares. Instead of a smile and greeting, his friends and neighbors either became confrontational or turned away. This shunning was the worst part for him, and sometimes he saw knots of folks on the street talking among themselves and then looking at him as if *he* were guilty of the crime.

He reminded his deputies, whom he hoped would tell their friends, that if murders weren't solved within the first forty-eight hours, they could be the most difficult of all crimes to solve. The deputies, too, were getting hassled by their friends and neighbors.

At his desk at the sheriff's office in Ozark, another small town about the size of Nixa, Dwight had only the initial reports from the examination of the Camaro and the autopsy findings to guide him. Interviews with those who'd known Jackie had just been launched and would take weeks to complete. McNiel saw to it that a polygraph reader was installed in a third-floor office to be available if needed during the investigation.

Everyday, he pored over the reports. Gene Gietzen had supervised the processing of the Camaro. He ran the laboratory of the Springfield Police Department, which shared jurisdiction because the part of the lake where Jackie was found was within Springfield city limits. Gietzen's team had found a partial fingerprint on the small bulb of the Camaro's dome light, and the lens itself was missing.

The partial print was sent to the FBI to be compared to other fingerprints in a then relatively limited national database of known felons. Even if a match existed somewhere within the fledgling system, it would take days or even weeks to find it. In fact, most of the fingerprint comparisons were done not by computer but by technicians who used magnifying glasses to review them.

Gietzen's team also collected numerous hair samples from the Camaro, along with blood samples, and there were plenty to choose from—dozens of sites were found inside the car, with most of the blood located in the backseat. It seemed to have come from the driver's-side area, and all the samples matched Jackie's blood type (this was in an era before widespread DNA analysis, so blood type matching was the best they could do). While some of the hairs didn't match Jackie's, without a suspect to compare them to, the hairs weren't much good as evidence.

Incredibly, Gietzen's team came up with a list of 189 items he found in the Camaro—everything from a

Doublemint gum wrapper and a seven-month-old McDonald's receipt to Jackie's Wilson Fieldmaster glove she took to softball games. There was a vial of Aziza eye shadow, a top from a can of Aqua Net hair spray, two bars of Zest soap, and four plastic containers of blush. There were two umbrellas, a bottle of Tropical Blend Dark Tanning Oil, and matches marked "Cajun's Wharf." There was a St. Patrick's Day card signed "Cody," which was found in a special place below the dash. Every item was placed in a plastic bag containing a filing number and a brief description.

Earlier that day, McNiel had piloted a borrowed Piper Cherokee to fly to Columbia, Missouri, the home of the University of Missouri, 180 miles north of Christian County. He was then driven to Veterans' Hospital to observe while Dr. Jay Dix performed the autopsy.

McNiel had stopped just outside the door that led to the examination room, then forced himself to calm down. Sure, he'd watched dozens of autopsies, but this was different. It was the first one where he knew the deceased. Of course he realized that Jackie herself wasn't there. That Jackie was back in Nixa, in her mother's heart and deeply missed at the Sale Barn Café.

McNiel steadied himself and stepped forward. There, on a stainless steel table, lay the corpse. "I have to think of this as evidence," he told himself. "I can't forget that the most important thing in my life at this moment is finding evidence so I can put away whoever did this to her."

The autopsy hadn't produced any surprises, but it had

confirmed some grim suspicions. Dr. Dix had found facial swelling and superficial lacerations to the vaginal area, eyelids, lip, nose, and chin. His report listed bruising on both arms, on both legs, and on the chest. Four deep cuts were noted near the right ear. But the cause of death was clearly a skull fracture caused by a heavy object that gouged a deep hole in Jackie's right temple.

Afterward, McNiel knew it was time to call a meeting at the sheriff's office in Ozark. He studied the reports and photos from the autopsy and from Gietzen's examination of the Camaro. The next day, he met Sergeant Tom Martin and Detective Rodney Burk of the Springfield Police Department. Seeing Martin, McNiel relaxed a little. It was good to have him on the case. The Missouri State Highway Patrol investigations supervisor and his nine-member team were always juggling several homicide investigations. McNiel knew that Martin had plenty of practice in catching killers, and he knew his investigation would benefit from his colleague's experience.

Dwight McNiel and Rodney Burk shared the jurisdiction, and it was a team McNiel was happy to have at his disposal. Burk, another friend of McNiel's, had assisted him with various cases in Christian County and Springfield, and Burk knew his city. Maybe they'd have results sooner than expected, but in cases like this, unexpected twists and turns would become the norm, rather than the exception.

The three men began with looking over the autopsy report.

"That had to be from the jack," McNiel ventured, passing to the other men a set of eight-by-ten color glossies from the autopsy, showing the severity of Jackie's head wounds. "The bastard must have beaten her unconscious, thrown her on the ground, and used her own bumper jack to club her," McNiel continued, his voice neutral. He didn't reveal much of what he was thinking, but all of them felt the same: Get the guy who did this and lock him up to rot away the rest of his life.

"It had to be the lip of the jack because it wasn't a downward swing. It was from the side," Martin agreed.

"Like a golf swing," added McNiel, studying the photo.

Dr. Dix had also collected samples of blood, the contents of her stomach, head hair, pubic hair, an unknown substance from the right thumb, and a full set of vaginal swabs. He found semen and confirmed that Jackie had been raped. No big surprise, the trio agreed.

So far, there were no suspects. Two construction workers in a camper about a hundred yards from where Jackie's Camaro was found had been questioned, but they were soon ruled out as suspects.

One of the men, Larry Neal, recalled hearing the sound of a vehicle around 3 A.M. Looking out his window, he said he'd seen a dark car and a pickup truck about where the Camaro was found. He saw one person walk over to the pickup from behind the car and then drive off. Neal admitted he was too far away to identify the person, except to say it was probably a male. He was unable to identify the dark car regarding make, model, or license number.

"Looks like he beat her up inside the car and when he got her outside, he raped her," McNiel told the others as he continued scanning the photos.

The three investigators were facing a real challenge. What had led to this grisly murder? Because most of the victim's blood was found in the backseat, it indicated that Jackie was still alive while sitting back there. However, leaves and twigs were also found on the seat. Did that mean Jackie had been beaten inside the car until she became unconscious and unable to resist her killer? Was she then dragged outside the car and sexually assaulted? Then brought back inside and perhaps driven to Lake Springfield where her body was thrown?

"She must have been alive when she was in the rear seat," McNiel reasoned, "because dead bodies don't bleed." The question then became, was Jackie beaten and then thrown on the ground and raped? Did the killer then put her back in the car and drive to the lake to dump her body? And when the killer got to the lake, did he then strike her with the bumper jack that killed her?

The examination of the Camaro showed that the steering wheel was slightly bent and the driver's-side headrest was nearly snapped off. This suggested that Jackie, or someone who had been driving the car, had struggled mightily.

"Jesus, she fought like hell," McNiel muttered, unwilling to let the images become fully formed in his mind. Martin paused in his reading of the autopsy and looked over at Burk, who stopped taking notes on a yellow notepad. McNiel said, his voice low, "We need to know where he actually put her in the lake."

"Someone must've seen something. Everybody in town knew that girl's car!" The three men came up with a tentative plan. First they'd send investigators door-to-door in the area where the Camaro was found, as well as near the shoreline where the body was retrieved. They would also question deliverymen and store owners, and check that night's routine police reports.

In Nixa, McNiel's deputies would contact everyone who knew Jackie or had had recent contact with her, which would create a timeline of sightings that could lead to the killer.

Burk would take over the job of obtaining a "drift study" from the Missouri Department of Natural Resources; this would tell them how far Jackie's body had floated before it hooked onto vegetation near the boat ramp. If they knew the exact spot where the killer had come to the lake to dispose of the body, they might find something. If they were really lucky, they might find some tire tracks.

CHAPTER 7

--- ━━━━━━━━━━ ---

THE LION AND THE LAMB

A year and a half before Jackie Johns disappeared, Chief Deputy Dwight McNiel decided to wear a wire when he left his home one January 1984 night for an unexpected meeting with his boss, Christian County sheriff Buff Lamb.

It was an odd precaution for a lawman about to meet another lawman, but Lamb had told McNiel to show up at a turnaround on the side of a remote county road, *and to bring all his issued equipment.* Even for Sheriff Lamb, this was a weird—and somewhat alarming—request. But Buff Lamb was unconventional. McNiel didn't fear that he was headed for a violent showdown. No, something else was up, and he suspected it might be connected to local politics. McNiel figured Lamb was about to fire him. Why else would he tell his deputy to bring his issued gear?

McNiel knew his boss well and was immediately

suspicious of his intentions. Was he being set up for something? Would Sheriff Lamb renege on his promise of political support? He decided he should have a record of what Lamb might have to say.

Buff Lamb had long held the title to being southwestern Missouri's most eccentric lawman. A onetime rodeo rider and motorcycle daredevil turned sheriff, he'd won four elections in twenty years. Rowdy teens feared Buff, likening him to the tough Sheriff Buford Pusser in the movie *Walking Tall*. Locals regaled outsiders with stories about how Lamb used a heavy flashlight to whack lawbreakers upside the head to keep them in line. And he had a reputation as a ladies' man, marrying at least four times, an achievement that stood out among some members of the conservative Christian County.

At sixty-one, he was enjoying life with his most recent wife. But he'd promised McNiel and the public that he wouldn't run in the 1984 election and would instead support Dwight's bid to be elected sheriff. Lamb had confided one day to his deputy, "I've had enough. It's time to turn over the department to new blood."

In fact, that was why McNiel had agreed to take the deputy's job. Both men had agreed that this could be a logical step up for Dwight to take over the top spot.

Lamb was sitting in his cruiser when McNiel showed up, and to his surprise, the sheriff had activated his unit's flashers, the red and blue lights stabbing across the snow like a strobe in a disco.

As McNiel climbed out of his car, so did Lamb, and the two men faced each other in the snow. McNiel had a feeling this was not going to be one of those warm and fuzzy male bonding experiences. Three possibilities came to mind as McNiel faced his boss. The first—and preferred—possibility was that Lamb might actually keep his word. Maybe he'd called the roadside meeting to pass on words of wisdom about how to run the department. Or maybe he'd share a deep, dark secret about bodies buried somewhere in the thicket of Christian County Republican politics.

But what McNiel really suspected was plain old grassroots-style political treachery: Lamb was about to go back on his word!

Corinne, the latest Mrs. Lamb, probably had something to do with it. She undoubtedly liked being the wife of a sheriff, which was not the same as being the wife of a retired sheriff.

And sure enough, that was the deal.

"I've changed my mind. I'm going to run again," Lamb announced without preamble or apology.

But McNiel wasn't about to take this lying down. "Look, everyone knows you're planning to step down."

"Sorry, Dwight," the older man replied firmly. "That's how it is, and that's what's gonna be."

Aware of the pull of the recording device taped to his stomach, McNiel spoke clearly and calmly. "Buff, I haven't done anything wrong. You're the guy changing the rules," he pointed out. "You're the one who said you weren't gonna run again. You're the guy going back on his word."

"Don't matter. Don't matter at all. I'm gonna be sheriff again and you're gonna be gone, unless you want to publicly renounce the idea that you'd ever go up against me."

"And that won't happen," affirmed McNiel.

"Then we're done talking. Gimme your stuff. Put it right on the hood, right there. I don't want you stealing anything."

"Steal anything?" Now, McNiel felt his indignation rise. Steal something! Like all Christian County deputies, he'd been required to buy his own squad car and then lease it back to the county at twenty-one cents a mile. He'd bought his own gun, bullets, and uniforms. About the only thing he'd used in the way of borrowed equipment was his unit's radio, some assorted web gear, and a few cans of Mace. He would never forget the meeting or what was said.

Now, he slowly placed the Mace and the web gear on the hood of Lamb's squad car. He told Lamb he'd remove the radio from its mounting brackets the next morning and bring that to him as well.

"That's all? You sure?" said Lamb.

"You got it, Buff. See you in August."

"August?"

"The primary," McNiel reminded him. "I'm going to kick your ass, you old son of a bitch."

"We'll see about that. Others have tried," Lamb scoffed. Then, he got back into his cruiser and drove off.

———

In the days that followed, minus a paycheck, Dwight McNiel was forced to support his family by dipping into their modest savings. He began to wonder if getting mixed up in politics was really the wisest decision after all.

But his close friends—Bruce Harris, who was running for county circuit court clerk, and county prosecutor Tim McCormick—encouraged him to face down his rival. Both told him not to worry; he'd get the sheriff's job and the pay that came with it. The three of them just had to plot the right political strategy. And they believed that Buff Lamb was ripe for the picking.

They all knew Buff was confident that he would again be elected—after all, so far, he'd never lost. His reputation (he was either feared or loved, depending on your level of respect for the law) had been his trump card at the polls. Either way, it translated into votes. Lots of folks loved hearing stories about good old Buff rapping a six-cell flashlight across some miscreant's head. It made them feel safe.

Besides, political rebellion was virtually unknown in Christian County among Republicans, and Lamb didn't take McNiel's threat to whip him in the primary at all seriously. In fact, there hadn't been a primary in so long, he didn't think McNiel would even file with the county election department.

But he was wrong.

McNiel and Harris joined with the fiery, red-haired Tim McCormick, the county's closest version of a leprechaun, to down a few beers and design their political strategy. They decided to have fun with Lamb, going door-to-door and telling the voters that Buff Lamb was over the hill and way past his prime. They would point out that crime was picking up in the county because of the methamphetamine drug trade, and to counter that took a younger man with new ideas—a man like Dwight McNiel.

They'd also remind voters that flashlights upside a prisoner's head wouldn't stop crime. And if the talk got around as to how many times Lamb had been married, well, they wouldn't discourage such conversation. After all, it was a free country and a man could marry as many women as he wanted, one at a time.

And folks were free to talk about it, too, especially when they're devout, churchgoing citizens.

In August, Dwight McNiel won the county Republican primary over Buff Lamb two to one—which sent an enraged Lamb out to the voting precincts on a treasonous mission. He urged loyal Republicans to vote for the Democrat whom McNiel would face in the November election.

It was close in November, but McNiel won again. Now, at age thirty-two, he was the youngest sheriff ever elected in Christian County. Lamb had been eight years older when he had been first elected in 1965.

McNiel had kept his secret recording from his roadside encounter with Lamb as insurance against any of Lamb's possible claims that he had left the job in disgrace. But he hadn't needed the recording after all. Lamb hadn't spent much time on the campaign, figuring his reputation would be enough to best a politically inexperienced newcomer.

What Lamb hadn't counted on was the skilled political support that came from McNiel, Harris, and McCormick: the "Scotch/Irish Syndicate" as they called themselves.

While Lamb relied on driving around while on duty

to politick in his sheriff's department car, rebel Republicans went door-to-door after work explaining how important it was, given the rampant methamphetamine violence breaking out in the countryside, for a sheriff to mobilize against this threat.

Dwight McNiel was a young, good-looking candidate with a nice family. And in a county with the name "Christian," a lot of regular churchgoers were uneasy that Buff Lamb had just married his seventh wife, who was about the right age to be his daughter.

On January 1, 1985, the day he officially took office, Dwight told his wife, Susan, "I'm going to change the world." He adjusted his badge in a mirror. He wanted it just right. Then he put on his sheriff's Smokey Bear hat and adjusted it so it was just right, too.

The night before, he had reached out to Lamb with a phone call.

"Let's let bygones be bygones. Let's make this change go smoothly," he had said.

"No, hell no," was Lamb's answer.

Just after midnight, McNiel walked up the stairs to the sheriff's department in the old courthouse in Ozark, where he had lived since he was a boy. He had a ring of keys in his pocket. He felt it would be a great day, New Year's Day. The first day for Sheriff Dwight McNiel.

It was a trip he had made hundreds of times since becoming chief deputy three years earlier. But what he saw when he opened the familiar door to the sheriff's office shocked him. What he saw looked like the aftermath of a burglary.

All the furniture except for the chair dispatcher Lana Sackett was sitting on was gone. The evidence locker, a small room guarded by a wire mesh door, was empty. Except for three radios sitting on the floor beside Sackett, who looked tearfully at her new boss, the former squad room had been stripped bare. Even the clock was gone.

In cells in the back, nine hungry prisoners stared out morosely from cells so foul that the odor was gagging. McNiel hadn't seen the offices since Lamb had fired him a year earlier, and he knew that his first official act was to calm a distraught Sackett down.

"I didn't dare try to call you," she said, still in tears. "Buff would have fired me on the spot. I need this job."

"Don't worry about it, Lana," he said. "You're still my dispatcher."

Disgusted, but determined not to show it, McNiel went downstairs and used a phone in an unlocked office to arrange for the prisoners to be immediately taken to another county jail until he could get his own jail and offices cleaned and reoutfitted.

Exterminators arrived on New Year's Day and gassed the legions of roaches in the jail, causing them to flee in all directions. This led to an uproar among employees on other floors when they showed up for work the next day and found that bugs had moved in. But political upheaval usually comes with a price.

And yet, until Jackie Johns's body was found in Lake Springfield nearly six months later on June 22, a kind of cease-fire had seemed to descend over Christian County.

Bullet-riddled corpses were showing up every few days along stretches of lonely dirt roads in counties all around, but Christian County had unexpectedly been spared.

On June 18, 1985, when the Jackie Johns case began with the discovery of her car, Sergeant Tom Martin had quipped to McNiel, "Well, son, it's finally your turn. You've got to admit it—you've been pretty darn lucky so far."

CHAPTER 8

A SUSPECT

From the Christian County Crime Stoppers log, June 23, 1985 (male caller):

> I don't want my name used. Don't trace this. I got information. It's about that girl from the lake. I saw someone I know on the same night the paper said she disappeared. It was at the 7-11. Gerry Carnahan. He was in his old Chevy truck parked in their lot when that girl went inside. He just sat there with his lights out. The bastard was watching for that girl. That's a fact. You need to check it out. Carn-a-han. I don't want the reward.

On Monday, June 24, two days after Jackie's body was found, Gerald Carnahan was due at 1 P.M. at the sheriff's office in Ozark. After the anonymous call claiming Carnahan had been parked behind the 7-11, a deputy had contacted him and asked him to come in for questioning. Carnahan quickly agreed.

McNiel waited at his desk on the third floor of the courthouse in Ozark. With him were Tom Martin of the Highway Patrol, who had helped to retrieve Jackie's body from Lake Springfield, and Detective Rodney Burk from the Springfield Police Department. They had met intentionally early so that they could discuss the forthcoming interview with Carnahan.

Now, McNiel leaned back in his swivel chair, mulling over his approach to this highly unusual suspect. He told Martin and Burk that Gerry Carnahan was the son of Garnett Carnahan, owner of Springfield Aluminum and said to be the richest man in Nixa. Garnett lived in an elaborate compound at the end of a private drive.

But Gerry, despite having a good job at his father's company, drove an old Chevy pickup with a bad muffler. It was a particularly unusual kind of truck, a 1961 Chevrolet Apache, blue over white with spoked wheels. A strange choice, since he could easily have had a new Cadillac.

Earlier that day, McNiel checked motor vehicle registrations through the Missouri Department of Revenue in Jefferson City, the state capital. A clerk could locate only two blue over white '61 Apaches registered in southwestern Missouri—and one belonged to Carnahan.

The first time Dwight McNiel laid eyes on Gerald Carnahan was in September 1984, at a fund-raiser McNiel had organized to raise money for his bid to become sheriff of Christian County. McNiel told Martin and Burk that Carnahan had made a memorable entrance at the Riverside Inn when he showed up with his new wife, Patricia Collins. She had attended high school in Ozark about the same time as McNiel. Collins was thirty-eight and had married Gerry, twenty-seven, a year earlier.

The sheriff told the other two cops that it seemed as if Pat had shown up towing Gerry, rather than the other way around. She had caused a big fuss among the gossips of Christian County when she married a much younger man. But even hardened rumormongers grudgingly admired her.

Although she was nearly twelve years older than her husband, Pat Collins was beautiful and smart, and very much her own woman. She had become a single mother in high school, but went to college, where she earned a master's degree in public administration. That landed her a job as director of the county's public aid office. And because county jobs meant paying political dues, it was a good move for Collins to show up at a fund-raiser, especially for the benefit of a guy who seemed a shoo-in for sheriff.

By that time, McNiel had already wiped out longtime sheriff Buff Lamb in the Republican primary, and since a Democrat hadn't won the office of Christian County sheriff in decades, the election seemed to be a lock, and victory for McNiel was in the air.

"I remember that Gerry showed up with long hair and a flashy suit and, I think, this Louis Vuitton scarf thing. He shook hands with everybody," McNiel recalled. "Pat's a real good-looking woman," he said, "and I told her

I was happy for her, marrying a handsome younger man."

McNiel also knew there was a third person who lived with them at the old house on South National Avenue, built on several acres that used to be part of a farm where cattle were raised and corn was grown. That person was Sara, Pat Collins's daughter. On the day the three investigators waited for Carnahan to show up to be questioned, Sara was turning twenty, the same age as Jackie Johns. Carnahan was not asked whether there had been a party for his stepdaughter.

Now, McNiel pushed Gerry Carnahan's criminal records printout across the table. It was slight; he'd only racked up a few traffic tickets and one drunken driving charge.

McNiel was somewhat apprehensive; he had no idea what to expect from Carnahan. He had heard that some of the young waitresses down at the Sale Barn Café called him "creepy." If he ate at the café, he must have known Jackie. The place was a magnet for meetings and hookups.

The day before, a waitress told McNiel that Gerry liked to stare at the women, particularly Jackie, and always seemed to have that faint smile on his face. He didn't try to grab any of them, she admitted, and to her knowledge, he hadn't followed any of them after work. But everyone who spoke about the man they knew as "Gerry" agreed that his smile was unnerving. There was something just not right about a man who always seemed to be amused, as if he were in on some secret joke.

Because of the anonymous call the police had received, backed up by another witness who said that he, too, had seen a truck that looked like Carnahan's pickup behind the 7-11 when Jackie was last seen entering the store, Gerry Carnahan was shaping up to be the prime suspect. But he wasn't the only suspect.

It was too early for that, and other leads were still being investigated.

McNiel scanned Carnahan's mug shot. It had been taken when he'd been arrested for drunk driving and revealed a man with Elvis-style hair and a young Jackie Gleason's face. And there was that unsettling smile, even in his mug shot. It almost seemed as if Carnahan was always aware that his father's money and influence would get him out of any trouble.

McNiel heard footsteps on the stairs and turned toward the door to his office. He watched it open just enough to see a hand, but then the door shut and someone knocked.

McNiel got up and opened the door to find Carnahan standing there, alone. That was a surprise, since McNiel had thought for sure that a businessman of Carnahan's stature would bring a lawyer. But then, Carnahan seemed like an odd bird. McNiel still couldn't figure out why a successful businessman would drive a twenty-four-year-old truck that needed fixing up.

"Gerry, thanks for coming in," McNiel greeted him. "Sit down, please," he said, waving casually to a straight-backed wood chair with no armrests. A tape recorder preserved an exact record of what was said.

Burk and Martin sat on folding chairs near a conference table just a few feet from Carnahan.

"Thank you," Carnahan said, smiling and settling into the chair.

Uh-oh, thought McNiel. Right away, he sensed trouble. If his suspect was going to be polite and cooperative, the interrogation would be tough. McNiel preferred nervousness, or at least annoyance. If this guy was innocent, he ought to be irritated, or at least indignant that he was being asked if he had anything to do with the rape and murder of a young girl.

McNiel watched his suspect's hands, knowing that the guilty often signal their culpability by waving their hands when responding to questions, as if the motion might make their lies convincing. He had purposely seated Carnahan in a chair without armrests, knowing it could unsettle a guilty person.

But Carnahan simply folded his hands in his lap and kept his eyes on the sheriff's.

Checking him over, McNiel noticed that the knuckles on Carnahan's right hand were skinned and red, but he said nothing. Not yet.

"Know why you're here, Gerry?" he asked.

"I imagine it's about Jackie Johns," Carnahan replied easily.

"You still have a blue and white, older model Chevy pickup?"

"Yeah, I do. It's parked right out there. You're more than welcome to go through it and look at it," he offered, his eyes never leaving McNiel's.

"You already know that we got a call that you were parked at the 7-11 when Jackie Johns was there just a few minutes before. Weren't you up there behind the 7-11?"

"No," Carnahan denied, his expression pure innocence. "It wasn't me."

Martin and Burk gazed steadily at Carnahan, but he didn't flinch, keeping his eyes locked on McNiel's, as he continued to ask most of the questions.

"Okay. Well the information we have is that you might've been backed up there by the clubhouse looking back toward the 7-11. Three people say they saw you. Could somebody have borrowed your truck for anything? Could any of your relatives have taken it, maybe?"

"No," Carnahan replied. But then he began to introduce his alibi, which contradicted the Crime Stoppers caller. He said he'd spent most of that Monday night, when Jackie was last seen, with his stepdaughter, Sara. They'd gone to the Repair Shop, a restaurant in Springfield that served alcohol, but Sara, who was too young to drink spirits, drank soda pop. He had two beers and they ordered some tacos. Carnahan said several people should remember that they were there.

Then they drove back home to the farm for a short time, but left on separate errands, with Sara heading to K-Mart to find a curling iron. In fact, he said, Sara was a friend of Jackie's and had hoped to find her there. But Jackie wasn't scheduled to work that day.

Carnahan told the investigators that his next stop was at the Vara Warehouse, a storage business of his under renovation, where two friends were building shelves for the office. He brought some beer—a six-pack of Lowenbrau—chatted for about a half hour, and then went back to the farm where he and Sara watched the first part of *The Tonight Show Starring Johnny Carson*, which started at 10 P.M. Then they both went to separate bedrooms and fell asleep. That was it.

As the investigators looked at each other, he went on to say that his wife, Pat, was at Lake of the Ozarks attending a training conference for her job.

"I'm trying to think why somebody would think, you know, that my truck was up there behind the 7-11," Carnahan said easily.

"Apparently this person knows you," McNiel pointed out. "He knows you and your truck and said it was you and your truck. We have other witnesses, too, who didn't say 'it looked like you.' They said it *was* you."

Carnahan sat there, listening but showing no emotion.

"Did you know Jackie?" McNiel asked, knowing the answer.

"I sure did. She had worked at our facilities right after the strike situation. We replaced some people, and she worked there for, uh, about a month. Something like that."

"Okay. Did you ever date her socially or go out with her?"

"No, no," Carnahan said, looking surprised at the question.

"You just knew her from the plant?"

"Well, at the Sale Barn. You know, eating lunch, and you know, she'd wait on me and stuff. I knew her from there, as well. I'd say for quite some time I've known her."

"Do you know anything at all, Gerry, about her disap-pearance up there last Monday night?"

"Boy, I sure don't. I sure don't," Carnahan repeated.

"Let me make sure I have this straight," McNiel said. He stood and moved closer to Carnahan until he was standing over him, and Carnahan looked up and kept eye contact. "Monday night when you came in from visiting the Vara Warehouse. Sara was awake and up?"

"Yeah, I'm trying to think. I believe she was. Well, it's just kind of hard, you know, to think back and, uh, I feel confident that she was up. But I can't, you know, I can't say that she was or wasn't."

"You don't have any qualms about us taking finger-prints from you?"

"No," Carnahan said with the confidence of an inno-cent man.

"Are you left- or right-handed?" McNiel asked.

"Right-handed."

"I notice that you have some skinned places on your knuckles there. How'd you do that?" McNiel pointed out, hoping to rattle him.

"Oh, I got this right here at a volleyball game yes-terday."

"You guys play rough, don't you?"

"Well, we played seven games out in the heat," Car-nahan explained. "So yeah."

Burk moved from his chair and stood beside Carna-han. Both Burk and McNiel towered over their suspect, whose driving arrest data showed he was five feet nine inches and 165 pounds.

"Would you be willing to take a polygraph examination?" Burk asked.

Carnahan didn't hesitate for a minute. "Sure I will. Just call me and tell me when."

At the end of the interview, McNiel stood at a hallway window and watched Gerry Carnahan walk to his truck. The three enforcers had decided ahead of time that if he offered, they would not take him up on searching the truck. After all, the evidence was focused on Jackie's Camaro, and besides, if Carnahan was the killer, he'd had almost a week to clean his truck.

McNiel heard the old Chevy pickup start. It was loud, loud enough that legally he could have rushed down to his squad car, caught up with Carnahan, and pulled him over for excessive noise. But that would just entail a ten-dollar fine. The residents of Nixa were hollering for a murderer's head on a platter, not a ticket for a bad muffler. He'd be laughed out of town for that move!

Gerry Carnahan's polygraph was set for the next day in an office at the courthouse. McNiel had arranged for a polygraphist from the Springfield Police Department to be ready at a moment's notice, expecting that he might have to interview hundreds before getting a sense of who the killer might be.

But Detective Don Eskew of the Springfield Police Department got a call that morning from Carnahan saying that the polygraph was off. Apparently, Gerry's father, Garnett, had looked into the reliability of the tests and didn't like what he found. And Carnahan's attorney had also advised against it.

But nearly a month later, when McNiel and Burk were deep into the hundreds of interviews they would conduct in the Jackie Johns case, they received a surprising message from Gerry Carnahan. He called from his office at Springfield Aluminum in Nixa and said he needed to see them both right away.

The two men found Carnahan at his desk in a short-sleeved shirt and tie, looking unexpectedly haggard. And before the interview ended, he admitted he was taking strong nerve medication prescribed by a doctor.

To their surprise, Carnahan wanted to talk about a crime. Not Jackie's murder, but an extortion attempt against him. He told McNiel and Burk that he had received a telephone call from a man whose voice he didn't recognize. The caller wanted $25,000 and gave Carnahan forty-eight hours to come up with the money. If he didn't, the caller warned, he would contact police and tell them he'd seen Carnahan's pickup truck parked behind Jackie's car on Highway 160 on the night of her disappearance.

Well, this was an interesting twist, McNiel thought, especially since the media hadn't reported that a witness was interviewed the day after Jackie's body was found and said he had seen a pickup truck and a dark car near the spot where her Camaro would be found. The witness was Larry Neal, one of the two construction workers questioned earlier and ruled out as suspects. Neal was living in a camper trailer a hundred yards off Highway 160 and, for some reason, woke up about 3 A.M. He said he happened to look out toward the highway and saw a pickup truck parked behind a dark car right at the area where Jackie's car was found later that morning. He hadn't seen the Camaro. The construction worker provided only a sketchy description of each vehicle and thought the pickup might have been tan. The best he could do on the car was that it was a dark color and a compact. He said the pickup drove off first, leaving him suspicious that someone had stolen some gas from the car. But then, the dark car had driven away too.

Maybe there really was an extortionist who really did see a truck on Highway 160 where Jackie's car was found, theorized McNiel initially, but even though Neal's description of the pickup was vague, it didn't seem like it could have been Carnahan's blue over white '60s Chevy truck. And how would Carnahan know about Neal's report? And why would he bring it up even if he did know? The whole thing didn't make sense. It sounded fishy. McNiel and Burk would later agree that Carnahan had made it all up, most likely in a clumsy attempt to try to throw off police and make them believe a would-be extortionist was the killer.

"Well, we'll check into this matter," McNiel assured Carnahan, "but you've got to cooperate." McNiel offered to put a trap on Carnahan's phone line, which could lead them to the sinister caller. In fact, he could have it done that day.

Gerry Carnahan seemed to mull it over, and while they had him there, the investigators tried to get him to recall what he'd been doing on the night Jackie disappeared, but Carnahan wanted no part of a polygraph and turned down their offer to put a tap on his line. He did say that he knew that an acquaintance of his, Allyn Wollard, had been the person who called Crime Stoppers claiming to have seen Carnahan's pickup. But he said the so-called extortionist hadn't sounded like Wollard.

Wollard had been a friend of Carnahan's, but the relationship had turned sour after a strike at Springfield Aluminum, he told McNiel and Burk. Wollard had walked the picket line and hollered an obscenity, Carnahan said, when he had driven by the picket line.

"You might want to get a second opinion about taking the polygraph test," Burk suggested. "You know, you want to be totally cooperative in this investigation. The homicide of a young girl—this is an emotional community issue. People will not stop talking until we have the killer. And right now they're talking about you."

CHAPTER 9

NOTHING

The next step in the investigation was to question Gerry Carnahan's wife, Pat Collins. However, Collins hadn't been in town when Jackie Johns disappeared; indeed, she was still away at a conference in Lake of the Ozarks, a Missouri resort town. But she was married to their top suspect, so she was automatically included on the list of persons to be interviewed.

Carnahan's alibi witness, his stepdaughter Sara, would also be crucial to their investigation. But there was no hurry there. Sheriff Dwight McNiel and Sergeant Tom Martin of the Highway Patrol wanted to gather as much information as they could before they questioned Sara about where Gerry Carnahan was on the night that Jackie was believed to have been killed. That way, they could find holes in her story, if there were any holes.

On the two-hour trip to Lake of the Ozarks, Martin

relaxed while McNiel, sitting next to him, was about as tense as he could remember. This was his first big murder case as sheriff of Christian County, and unlike Martin, he had not yet learned to adjust to the pressure.

They headed east on Interstate 44 toward Lake of the Ozarks.

"Carnahan was there. He had to be," Martin suddenly spoke up, echoing McNiel's own thoughts.

They had been over the witness statements time and again, and at least three witnesses put Gerry Carnahan in his truck at the rear of the 7-11 around 11 P.M. that Monday, June 17. Adding to their conviction that they had their man, Carnahan had backed off from his agreement to take a polygraph.

Gerry Carnahan was now their prime suspect.

Martin was confident that McNiel had come to the right conclusion. The way they saw it, Jackie had gone to buy hair spray and cigarettes around 11 P.M., maybe five or ten minutes before. That seemed incontrovertible, and the timeline was pretty solid. Witnesses put Carnahan there at the same time, too. So if he wasn't there, as he insisted, why wouldn't he just take the lie detector test and be done with it?

But Carnahan wasn't the only suspect. Other leads were being checked out, but so far they had gone nowhere. Larry Neal, a highway construction worker who had been sleeping in a camper at his job site just off Highway 160, said that early in the morning on Tuesday, June 17, a few hours after midnight, he heard a vehicle slow down and got out of bed. He said he thought that someone was trying to steal gas from what looked like a dark-colored Camaro parked out on 160. He said he got into his own pickup and drove closer, so that he saw enough of the Camaro to later tell police it could have been Jackie's car.

Neal told McNiel and other investigators that he'd gotten close enough to the truck to see that its interior dome light was on. However, he couldn't recall much about the driver except to say it was a white male wearing a short-sleeved shirt with the collar turned up. He also told investigators that he thought the guy drove a new model pickup dark in color, but couldn't identify it further than that. He also said he saw a small car in front of the Camaro that drove off before he got a close look at it, but he recalled that it was a dark-colored compact. Neal was ruled out as a suspect.

Another passerby told the investigators that he saw a small, dark-colored car, a pickup, and the Camaro but didn't get a good look at the drivers. However, this witness said he thought he saw a blond, heavyset woman standing near the front of Jackie's Camaro and a man he couldn't describe standing to the rear of it. He didn't recognize either person.

At the Lebanon exit, Martin turned north on a two-lane road that led through some of Missouri's prettiest hill country. It was about sixty miles to Lake of the Ozarks, the name of both the lake and the adjacent bustling resort village. Martin and McNiel were now headed for the Holiday Inn where Collins had agreed to take time from her conference to talk with them.

When they got to the hotel, they found her waiting in the lobby. Martin immediately noticed that she didn't smile or offer to shake hands. Instead, she sat down at a small conference table and asked, "All right. What do you want?"

Martin wasn't surprised by her attitude; after all, she was ready to defend her husband. Gerry Carnahan had not been arrested. He had only been questioned for about thirty minutes, and aside from three witnesses who claimed they saw his truck, including one who might have been settling a grudge, there was nothing to link him to Jackie's murder. At least, nothing yet.

Martin began. "Do you mind if I call you Pat?" he asked, taking the role of good cop.

She shook her head no and waited for him to continue.

"We have to ask you some questions, you know. Part of the investigation. We aren't accusing Gerry of anything, but we need to get some things cleared up."

"What things?" she asked tersely.

"Well, right now we have three witnesses who put your husband at the 7-11 about the same time as Jackie Johns was there. And we have your husband denying that he was there. We believe that the witnesses are telling the truth."

"Also, Pat, he was parked in the back along the side with his headlights out, like he was looking for somebody," McNiel added.

"If he's saying it wasn't him, I believe him," Collins said staunchly, clearly aligning with her man.

"Pat, why would those people lie?" Martin asked gently. "That old truck really stands out, and every one of them described that particular truck."

"Ask them why they would lie. I don't know," Collins said. "Maybe they did see an old truck. There are lots of pickups in Nixa, and lots of old pickups. You know that," she argued. She fixed Martin with a cold stare, daring him to contradict her.

"That's probably so," Martin agreed, waiting.

"There's no way Gerry's involved in this. No way," she said firmly.

The two lawmen asked Collins about the state of her marriage, but she wouldn't talk about it except to say there weren't any problems. Martin and McNiel wanted her to talk about the age difference between her and her husband, but she responded angrily to any questions on that subject. Martin knew there were doors in every person's psyche that, once opened with the right questions, could reveal a great deal. But Pat Collins was not going to allow any of her buttons to be pressed.

"Gerry wouldn't hurt anyone," she said. "He's sometimes naive and people try to take advantage of him, but he didn't have anything to do with this. He's not like that. You're wasting your time and mine."

"He knew Jackie," McNiel said, opening the connection between the two.

"Everybody in Nixa knew Jackie," Collins said. "That narrows it to about two thousand people. She was the Sucker Day Queen last year. She waited tables. Hundreds of men knew her. So what?"

When the questioning got around to her daughter, Sara, Collins became even more hostile. She reminded them that her daughter was a college student with good grades and absolutely no criminal record. "If Gerry had gone out again after 10 P.M., Sara would have said so," she affirmed. "I mean, what more do you want from her?" Collins asked with exasperation.

The interview took only a few minutes, and finally, Pat Collins stood and, without looking at it, accepted Martin's business card. She nodded when he asked her to call if anything about Jackie's murder came up, and then she turned without a word and walked off.

"Well, we sure struck out with her," McNiel said.

"That's an understatement," agreed Martin. But neither man was surprised. In fact, they'd pretty much expected that someone from the Carnahan clan might not want to be too cooperative.

On their return to Ozark, they stopped for coffee at a diner just off the interstate. Martin realized that McNiel was under intense pressure to find Jackie's killer, and knowing his friend, realized that unless they got really lucky and solved it quickly, this murder would eat at Dwight McNiel until all his waking moments would be defined by it.

Martin had already learned, somewhere around about his one hundredth homicide, that if you allowed a case like this to get to you, it would take over your life completely.

"That truck on 160," McNiel suddenly asked. "Did that construction worker see Gerry's truck behind Jackie's car? Do you think that's what he saw? He said that pickup looked like a newer model, but he was a hundred yards away. What about that?"

"That's something we've got to figure out," Martin agreed, "but I think we've got the right guy. We just need to wait."

In addition to the witnesses who claimed to have seen Carnahan's truck behind the 7-11, two other witnesses had come forward adamantly claiming that they'd seen Jackie's Camaro on Highway 160 around 3 A.M., with a dark-colored compact car parked in front of it, and a pickup parked behind it.

As the reports came in, the police became more and more frustrated. When would they get a clear bead on the man who had murdered Nixa's sweetheart and destroyed the town's innocence?

CHAPTER 10

PSYCHIC ASSISTANCE

Les and Shirley Johns were getting frustrated with what they considered a lack of results from the police department. It had been three weeks now, and still no arrest had been made. They agreed to meet with Highway Patrol sergeant Tom Martin at their trailer, where Martin tried to reassure them that the police were doing all they could.

But Les clearly had his doubts. Martin assured Les that police interviews were piling up, people were generally cooperating, and that, yes, there was a suspect. Although Martin said he couldn't talk about the evidence in the case, he did concede to Les that Gerald Carnahan was their prime suspect. In fact, he was their only plausible suspect. They just didn't have enough evidence to arrest him.

But Shirley shook her head. "I just don't know," she

said. "This waiting is so painful. It doesn't seem like you'll ever get him."

"We're not talking about a revenge killing," interrupted Les. "We're not talking about a love affair killing. We're talking about an ambush killing," he insisted, repeating what he often told friends and even strangers who had heard about Jackie and wanted to offer their support.

The community was firmly behind the family, as evidenced by a constant stream of letters of support, including many containing prayers for Jackie and her parents. But while they appreciated the support, the Johns family was impatient for an arrest and closure on Jackie's murder.

Although Sergeant Martin regularly visited the couple, Dwight McNiel stayed away, wounded by the animosity he'd felt from many in Nixa who believed he wasn't working hard enough to catch the killer. That was typical of this kind of case, but it hurt nonetheless. McNiel had committed himself to solving the case, no matter how long it took. But he couldn't make any missteps that would sabotage the apprehension of the murderer.

Then, in early July 1985, a day or so after one of Martin's visits, Shirley Johns received a telephone call at home. It was unlike any she had gotten since her daughter died. On the line was psychic Loretta Nichols, who said she had never before been in Nixa but had received visions showing her what had happened to Jackie. During the phone call, Nichols had talked about a large white wooden wheel with spokes outside of a restaurant that appeared in her visions. They had something to do with the man who killed Jackie. She asked Shirley if she could stop by the family's trailer and talk with her.

"Why not?" Les asked when he was told about the call.

At this point, Shirley was nearly out of hope. She knew that if a killer wasn't caught early, chances were good he wouldn't get caught at all. And nearly a month had passed since Jackie's death. But a psychic?

"Well, she might be able to help," she told Les. "Let's do it."

The middle-aged Loretta Nichols bore no resemblance to a turbaned crystal ball reader. About a week after her call, Nichols arrived at the Johnses' trailer and accepted a cup of coffee as the three settled into the living room. Remembrances of Jackie were all around them: There was the Sucker Day Queen tiara on a mantel, her softball trophies, and framed photographs of Jackie that occupied end tables and just about every other flat space.

There was also a newspaper clipping set in a plastic protector with a quotation from Jackie during her freshman year at Southwest Missouri State University. It read, "My favorite pastime is socializing. I love to go out and meet new people. College is more fun than high school because it seems that I meet a person every day that I never knew even existed."

Nichols held the photographs, studying each one. Shirley liked her, and was happy to have someone to talk to who seemed to possess special knowledge. Maybe this

Loretta person *could* see the future, or the past, or another world.

In a letter sent before her visit, Nichols had said that ideally she liked to visit a crime scene, "in all expectation of the triggering off of vibrations to get more information on the case," though in this instance, she wrote, she'd settle for access to Jackie's car since the actual murder site was unknown. Nichols, who said she had worked on unsolved criminal cases for years as a psychic, explained that she "saw" in her mind events that might or might not be connected to what happened to Jackie. If Nichols's vague psychic processes concerned Shirley, however, she didn't mention it at the time.

This is what Loretta Nichols said she "saw":

- "Jackie was hit on the right side of her head near or at the tip of the temple." The weapon was a "long, dark iron-type object, maybe a tool or jack handle."

- This happened "on a roadside beside a car."

- Nichols described seeing two young men. "One tall, thin, with longish curly or wavy auburn hair. The other stood more away. He wore shorts or trunks."

- Just before she was struck, Jackie said, "Oh, Greg or Craig."

- She bent down to pick something up and was struck five times, Nichols said.

Les was not impressed. Most of this information had been part of newspaper stories or broadcast reports. He began to shift in his seat.

Nichols pressed on with Shirley. One of the men "had a mole or birthmark near his nose." His nose was "strange," and she speculated that maybe it had been broken.

Then Nichols said, "I saw the letters CC with a slash across the middle." Though Nichols said she had no idea what this meant, she could easily have known it by simply reading news accounts, since it had been widely reported that Jackie's black Camaro was found pointing north on Highway 160 not far from its intersection with a county road called "CC."

Nichols concentrated again as Shirley watched raptly, but there were no further revelations.

A few days later, Nichols returned, this time with much more information. And these details were bizarre in the extreme. Nichols said she saw in her visions a "red Mustang" on the dark highway near Jackie's car. And in her most specific vision to date, she said she saw a "pale blue garter belt . . . shown to me hanging from the rear-view mirror" of the red Mustang.

There was also a silver medallion that had dropped to the road.

Then, a "stable or stall for horses" showed up in her mind. Nichols speculated that the glimpse of a stable might be purely symbolic and could somehow be connected to the term "stable" when it is used to describe a "pimp's stable of prostitutes."

Shirley didn't have any idea what these symbols might mean. Certainly, Jackie had not been involved with prostitution. And none of the witnesses so far had seen a red Mustang on the night Jackie had disappeared. Nor did Jackie possess a pale blue garter belt, at least as far as her mother knew.

Then, the psychic's visions became even more frightening. Nichols said she saw visions of Jackie lying under a haystack with only her right forearm sticking out. "Her hand was open," she emphasized.

The psychic told of seeing a pearl, and then told Shirley that it might mean the color "bluish gray" or "white," because those were the colors of pearls. But she didn't know what this vision was supposed to mean.

"Does it have to do with pearls or the colors of pearls?" asked Shirley. But Nichols said she didn't know.

She again envisioned the haystack and said this is where Jackie's body was hidden before she was placed in the lake. Then she told of hearing Jackie speak.

" 'You don't know what they did to me,' " Nichols told Shirley she heard in the audio portion of her visions. Then a man's booming voice, " 'We're going to make an example of her.' "

Shirley went from being enthralled to being frightened by the visions. It was tempting to believe them because they were so specific, but Nichols supplied no names or locations.

Then Nichols returned to her recurring vision of a "large wheel with spokes," painted white and made of wood. It was leaning up against a post, she told Shirley, and reminded her of a stagecoach wheel from the early West.

"Let's look in the phone book to see if there's a restaurant by that name," she suddenly urged, and they leafed through the pages of the phone book until they found that there was, in fact, a local restaurant named the Stagecoach Lounge.

It was in Springfield, a much larger city six miles to the north of Nixa.

Finally, on July 19, 1985, Nichols convinced Shirley they should look for evidence on their own. They drove along area roads close to the Johnses' trailer and stopped near the county road known as CC, which crossed Highway 160 not far from where Jackie's Camaro was found.

Close to the small road leading to Les and Shirley's trailer, the two of them searched a ditch where they found a brown plastic hairbrush with metal teeth and a white tube of Blistex lip balm.

Nichols was sure these items were connected to Jackie's murder, and Shirley got excited, but hours later she began to have doubts. What if they searched ditches on other roads nearby? Would they have found similar items?

Detective Rodney Burk of the Springfield Police Department, the other lead investigator on the case along with Sergeant Tom Martin and Sheriff Dwight McNiel, took the call from Shirley about what she and her psychic had found in the ditch. He collected the hairbrush and tube of Blistex, placing each carefully in separate labeled envelopes. Then he sealed each one. Burk canvassed homes in the neighborhood where the items

were found, but none of the neighbors remembered anything unusual. Finally, he sent the evidence to Gene
Gietzen at the Springfield Police Department crime lab
for testing.

Ultimately, nothing came of Loretta Nichols's visit or
her visions. But it did give Shirley a feeling—if fleeting—
of empowerment. She wasn't just sitting around doing
nothing, feeling helpless, as she had been ever since her
daughter had been found. No, Shirley Johns was determined to explore every possible option to find out what
had really happened to her daughter.

CHAPTER 11

- - - ———————— - - -

"PULL 'EM DOWN"

In the late summer and into the fall of 1985, Sheriff Dwight McNiel and investigators Sergeant Tom Martin of the Highway Patrol and Detective Rod Burk of the Springfield Police Department, among others, conducted interview after interview in their investigation of the murder of Jackie Johns, more than 150 in all. McNiel arranged for a police polygraphist to be stationed on the third floor of the courthouse in Ozark for quick access whenever an interviewee's story or details were doubted. But few tests were actually given.

Jackie's former boyfriends and dozens in the popular waitress's wide circle of friends, both women and men, were questioned. The details that turned up in the interviews didn't stray far. For instance, it seemed to be common knowledge that Jackie had somehow obtained a twenty-one-year-old woman's driver's license and had used it occasionally to buy beer. Stories about "The Jerk," the teenage-sounding boy who made obscene telephone calls to attractive young women all over town, were revealed by more than a dozen women who were interviewed. And dozens of young men said they believed Jackie confided in them, but only a few said they had ever been romantically involved with her.

McNiel ordered transcripts of the interviews. These were studied, and certain details and alibis for the night of June 17 when Jackie disappeared were thoroughly checked out. But nothing pointed beyond the investigation's prime suspect, Gerry Carnahan.

Finally, late in October, Sheriff McNiel received an alarming tip. One of his investigators told him that he had overheard a casual comment from a Carnahan family member stating that Gerry Carnahan intended to make a trip to Taiwan, via Los Angeles. McNiel already knew from his investigation of Jackie's death that Carnahan from time to time traveled to Taiwan on trips connected to the family's aluminum business. The Asian country was said to be a good source of cheap scrap aluminum that could be shipped to the factory in Nixa and melted down to make custom boat parts. But McNiel also knew that Taiwan was a country with no extradition treaty with the United States, and he figured that Carnahan was concerned that a Christian County grand jury might indict him for murder, and so wanted to flee to where he would be safe if that happened.

On October 31, 1985, McNiel confirmed through confidential sources that Gerry Carnahan was already on his way to Los Angeles, en route to Asia. McNiel quickly met with his friend Tim McCormick, the Christian County prosecutor. He asked what, if anything, they could do to get Gerry Carnahan arrested that very day.

What they came up with was this: At least three witnesses swore that Gerry Carnahan was in his pickup behind the 7-11 at about the same time that Jackie had been seen coming in to buy hair spray and cigarettes. Which meant that Carnahan must have been lying when he claimed he wasn't, McCormick determined, further claiming that lying to the police essentially supported a charge of tampering with evidence. And while legal scholars might have scoffed at such an idea, it was enough for them to get a warrant quickly typed up for a judge to sign. Once a judge signed that warrant, it would be valid even if the charge might later be laughed out of court. But where was the judge?

Like all criminal court circuits in Missouri, the circuit containing Christian County also included several other counties that would be part of a judge's responsibility. On this day, the on-duty judge was about thirty miles away in a courthouse in Taney County.

With lights flashing, McNiel sped in a county cruiser to Taney County, where he spent a frantic hour locating the judge. He finally succeeded both in tracking him down and getting him to sign the warrant, and McNiel immediately called the Los Angeles Police Department to request that Gerry Carnahan be arrested at the airport or wherever they could find him. He faxed a copy of the signed warrant to the L.A. cops.

Carnahan's arrest was perfect material for a Hollywood script. He had already boarded the flight to Taiwan and the local cops did not have jurisdiction to board the plane and haul him away. That was left to the FBI, who sent two agents racing to the airport to serve the warrant that had been faxed from Ozark, Missouri.

While the jet sat waiting for instructions from the tower, the agents were escorted by airport security to the tarmac and then driven to the aircraft. A truck brought a portable ramp that was placed against the plane's forward door. The FBI report stated that Gerry Carnahan had been seated in first class and was wearing a gray suit and dark tie. He offered no resistance when the Feds came for him.

Carnahan would later say that he had only intended to travel to Taiwan on business. His trip was *definitely* not a way to get out of Dodge before a Christian County grand jury came up with a charge with his name on it. But he did waive extradition, a legal move that would free him from the Los Angeles County jail as soon as someone from Missouri arrived to get him. And that happened a week later.

The "dos" and "don'ts" of the Men's Central Jail for Los Angeles County, according to advice in a 1985 letter to the editor of a California newspaper sent by an anonymous inmate:

"Dos: Act crazy, work out, pray, sleep with one eye open.

Don'ts: Don't let your poop sit, always flush right away! Don't drop the soap or stare at naked dudes in the shower room (you might get raped)."

Of the thousands of men held at the jail, many came from violent street gangs. The feuds and rivalries of the street carried over to the dorms, which held as many as a hundred men. L.A. County's Men's Central Jail was a dangerous and often violent place.

McNiel and his chief deputy Nick Corsentino had heard about the facility's reputation. It was one of the world's largest jail systems and, many said, the toughest. The men's portion of the jail was in downtown Los Angeles.

At the main entrance, the Missouri lawmen placed their firearms and ammunition in lockboxes and were ushered through a bewildering series of electronic doors.

Gerald Carnahan was waiting for them in a small conference room in a featureless gray hallway, and actually seemed relieved to see them. He'd been held for seven long days in a dormitory the size of a high school gym with gangbangers on cots all around.

McNiel and his deputy wasted no time. After checking Carnahan out of the jail, they drove directly to the airport and headed back to Missouri. Shortly after midnight on November 7, 1985, a Frontier Airlines jet touched down at the small airport in Springfield. When Carnahan, hands cuffed in front to a chain around his waist, stepped through the jet's door into the cool night air, a sheriff's department squad car, lights flashing, was waiting for him.

Now, Gerald Carnahan was news again.

So was Dwight McNiel.

Carnahan's family sprang him from jail the next day;

they quickly came up with the requisite $75,000 in cash. When he left Greene County Jail in Springfield, Carnahan was wearing a business suit and a crisp new dress shirt, and, of course, he smiled for the television cameras.

But Gerry Carnahan had been arrested and then bailed out only on the authority of the warrant signed by the judge down in Taney County. To make a stronger case, most county prosecutors then present a case to a grand jury, and this was done with the evidence-tampering charge. The grand jury, which convened in mid-December of 1985, returned an indictment against Gerry Carnahan for evidence tampering on January 23, 1986. State law then required another arrest, arraignment, and bail proceeding for the indictment.

With that second indictment in hand, Sheriff Dwight McNiel rode with Sergeant Tom Martin and went looking for Carnahan along Highway 160, the most direct route between Carnahan's residence in Springfield and his office at the family business in Nixa.

They headed north toward Springfield and soon passed the spot where Jackie Johns's Camaro had been found.

McNiel finally had what he believed would lead to an eventual arrest in the murder of Jackie Johns. It wasn't a murder warrant. But it was a felony warrant and it had Carnahan's name on it. It would be enough to lighten some of the public pressure for an arrest for murder in the Johns case. The $75,000 cash bond in the evidence-tampering case would ensure that Gerry Carnahan didn't flee the country before they could nail him for murder.

It would buy time for McNiel and Martin to find enough evidence for a murder charge.

Also, if potential witnesses saw that the county was serious about the only real suspect in the Jackie Johns case, witnesses unknown to McNiel and Martin, witnesses who could have crucial information, might come forward because of the publicity over the evidence-tampering charge.

"There he is," said McNiel, as just ahead, the car Carnahan was driving quickly pulled over in response to McNiel activating his emergency lights. Gerry Carnahan stepped out and asked innocently, "What's wrong?"

McNiel tersely told him to turn around and place his hands on the top of the police cruiser. He then patted him down and handcuffed him.

It was explained to Carnahan that because of the formal indictment he was being arrested again for the same charge, evidence tampering, and he would again be taken to jail, fingerprinted, and photographed because that's what state law required with an indictment. However, the $75,000 posted for his bond could again be used to cover his bail.

It was a well-documented arrest; once the media heard that an indictment having some connection to the Jackie Johns murder investigation was likely, every local television station had sent a team to shadow both McNiel and Martin. So did the Springfield newspaper and two radio stations.

First, the sheriff and the sergeant took Carnahan to the Greene County Sheriff's Department in Springfield, where he was fingerprinted using more advanced equipment than that available at the small Christian County Sheriff's Department in Ozark. On the return trip to Christian County, McNiel took the scenic route with Martin riding shotgun and Carnahan handcuffed in the back. As they approached a small access road leading to the shore of Lake Springfield, he slowed to a few miles per hour.

"Remember this, Gerry?" McNiel asked, referring to the results of the drift study that had been requested early in the investigation from the Highway Patrol forensic lab. It suggested that Jackie's body had floated in a straight line, east for about a mile, which put the place where the body had been thrown into the water about one hundred yards from the access road.

Dwight McNiel let the police vehicle inch along, but never came to a complete stop. Then he turned to look back at his suspect. So did Martin, who observed Carnahan behind his sunglasses. Although only in his midforties, Martin had already acquired the hard, no-nonsense look of someone who knew he'd been lied to thousands of times by professional liars.

So far, Carnahan had said nothing. In fact, during the entire flight back from Los Angeles, with a layover in Dallas, McNiel and his chief deputy Corsentino were amazed that Carnahan hadn't uttered a word, except to ask to use a bathroom.

But this was different. Two hard-nosed cops had him alone down by a lake. The media had ditched them in Springfield at the sheriff's department, likely realizing that the only thing left would be an uneventful and

routine transport to Christian County, where the indictment had been issued, where Carnahan would be released
on the same $75,000 that had been posted by his family
back in November.

And Gerry Carnahan must have realized that cops
who would go to the trouble of having the FBI drag him
off a plane in L.A. to bring him back to Missouri on a
pretty flimsy evidence-tampering charge must surely
believe that he had murdered Jackie Johns. Now, here he
was, handcuffed and completely at their mercy.

"You want to get it off your chest, Gerry? Maybe apologize to the family so we can all move on with our lives?"
McNiel asked his prisoner.

Carnahan looked at McNiel and then at Martin, then
quickly turned away and gazed out to where a patch of
the lake could just be seen.

"C'mon Gerry," said McNiel. "What do you think of
a man who would beat the crap out of a nice girl like
Jackie. Beat her bloody and then, when she was helpless
on the ground and couldn't lift a finger to help herself,
use a bumper jack to tee off on her head like he was
swinging a golf club? You want to talk about that?"

Carnahan kept silent. The Christian County jail,
where he was headed for final processing, was just a few
miles away, but it represented a relative haven. Once
there, he knew that his lawyer, who was awaiting his
arrival, would release him. Even if they increased his
bond, his family could afford to get him out. Carnahan
said nothing.

But McNiel wasn't finished with him.

"Right down there, that's where you put her in the water, Gerry. Right down that road. You know you did and we know it." The car crawled past the access road, giving them all a straight view down to the water.

"Her family is a mess over this, Gerry. Shirley has cried herself sick. She can't sleep. Les wants to blow your head off. Can you blame him?"

And then, his patience gone, McNiel demanded, "Look at me, damn it!"

But Carnahan wouldn't look. He clenched his fists and stared straight out over the cruiser's hood. He made no sound and seemed to barely breathe.

At the sheriff's office in Ozark, an evidence search warrant awaited them. It was signed by a Christian County judge and authorized police to take samples of Gerry Carnahan's hair and blood. The men led their prisoner into the office's Breathalyzer room where deputies took drunks for processing. In the room were a table and several chairs.

Deputy Danny Clinton joined McNiel and Martin as Carnahan's cuffs were removed. "Sit down," someone told him, and he did what he was told. McNiel showed him the warrant, but he didn't ask to read it. Instead, what happened next made all three investigators step back, stunned.

Suddenly, Gerry Carnahan leaped from the chair and flung himself into a corner of the small room where he curled into a fetal position. He began to scream, and then moaned and sobbed, muttering something unintelligible. It was as if he were possessed!

Dumbfounded, McNiel just stared as Martin shook his head.

Clinton, a weight lifter who could bench-press 350 pounds, stepped toward Carnahan, but the sheriff waved him back. Carnahan was sobbing so hard his chest heaved and he began wheezing, as if he were choking.

Was he having a heart attack? the observers wondered. And then, he was silent. For a long moment, everyone was speechless. Then, McNiel told him, "Get up, Gerry. Get up!"

McNiel grabbed him by the arm and led him back to the chair.

"Gerry, we're going to get these samples and we'll only use what force is necessary. We want you to cooperate. We don't want to use force but that's what we'll do if we have to. Do you understand?"

Carnahan refused to acknowledge the warning, so McNiel then motioned to Clinton, who lifted Carnahan to his feet and stood him against a wall. Another deputy stepped close and clipped his head hair. A medical technician, who was waiting in the hall, then came in and asked McNiel to roll up the sleeve on Carnahan's right arm. She quickly drew a vial of blood and left the room.

Clinton then pushed Carnahan back into the chair to await a male technician, wearing latex gloves. Gerry Carnahan eyed him fearfully.

"Take your pants down, Gerry," McNiel said. "Pull 'em down."

Carnahan reached for his belt buckle, and then hesitated. He appeared shocked at what was being requested.

Whatever fight had been in him drained away as Clinton pulled him, chair and all, to where the technician pointed.

"Pull 'em down to your knees," ordered McNiel.

Carnahan pulled his pants down to his knees.

"Now the underwear."

Carnahan froze. This was the ultimate indignity.

The technician pulled the shorts down far enough to expose pubic hair and passed a cheap plastic comb through the hair several times. Then he placed the comb and whatever it had picked up into a plastic evidence bag. He used scissors to snip other samples and placed them into another bag.

"All right, Gerry. Pull 'em up," said McNiel. "You're done for now. Your lawyer is waiting to talk to you."

CHAPTER 12

LIAR, LIAR

Gerry Carnahan's twenty-year-old stepdaughter Sara Collins shivered. It was a chilly Monday afternoon in late December 1985, nearly six months after Jackie Johns's murder and about ten days after the Christian County grand jury had been convened to look into the case. Her stepfather Gerry Carnahan was free on $75,000 bail on the evidence-tampering charge that had gotten him pulled off the plane in L.A. He had yet to be arrested a second time on the same indictment that he'd lied to the police when he insisted he had not been parked in his old Chevy pickup behind the 7-11 in Nixa at about the time Jackie was seen going inside the store. While she had heard her stepfather go on and on questioning the legality of such a charge and asking how denying that he had been somewhere could be construed as evidence tampering, he had not yet been indicted for anything. That was several weeks away.

Sara's statement to police that Carnahan had been at home with her the night Jackie was last seen, had the grand jurors believed it, could have potentially cleared Carnahan altogether on both the charge of evidence tampering and the suspicion of murder.

But she did not yet know it would be futile.

After parking her car outside the courthouse in Ozark, Sara pushed the heavy courthouse door open and stepped inside. A few feet ahead lay the stairs she had learned to dread. A few reporters were already hanging around, waiting for the next possible interview subject.

The stairs led up two floors to the wood-paneled courtroom the grand jury was using for the Jackie Johns murder investigation. It was the first grand jury convened in Christian County in at least fifty years. Old-timers said it was the first since the late 1800s. A jury of seven men and five women had been selected from a pool of forty-eight registered voters called to the courthouse.

Sheriff McNiel refused to speculate how long the jury would need to properly analyze the evidence of Jackie's murder and come up with a murder charge. A few days earlier, he said publicly, "They need to spend whatever time is necessary, whether it be six weeks or six days, to be sure that they have satisfied themselves that they have reviewed this case as thoroughly as possible."

The advantage of a grand jury over a police investigator, Dwight McNiel pointed out, was that a grand jury had "broad subpoena powers" that enabled them to question witnesses who might tell police they didn't want to talk.

Previously, it hadn't been necessary to first obtain a grand jury indictment to charge someone with a crime in Christian County. All that had ever been needed was for a cop to file criminal information. It was usually just the officer's word on paper that a crime had occurred and that a particular person was the probable perpetrator. This was based on a legal principle called "probable cause," which was enough to get a person in handcuffs and brought before a judge.

But after Jackie Johns was murdered, that changed. McNiel and the county prosecutor, Tim McCormick, pushed for a special grand jury to investigate the murder, and they found a judge who agreed to do so. A grand jury's proceedings are held in secret.

The day before, the *Springfield Leader & Press* had reported that the bigwigs of Christian County believed grand jurors would crack the Jackie Johns case, which had so far baffled the police. But, if there were no new witnesses, what had changed? What could a proceeding held in secret accomplish?

At the top of the steps, Jackie's parents, Shirley and Les Johns, would be waiting to see Sara Collins, who was the same age their daughter had been. They never missed a court hearing connected to their daughter's death. Like most folks in Nixa and throughout the Springfield area, Shirley and Les fervently believed that Sara was withholding the truth. It was awkward when she had to walk by them to open the grand jury room door.

The courtroom was off-limits except to grand jurors, the scheduled witness, and the prosecutor, McCormick. Not even Shirley and Les were allowed near the grand jury room. An armed deputy sheriff guarded the door as, according to the U.S. Constitution, a grand jury proceeding must be held in complete secrecy.

Sara was next up on the witness stand. It would be her third appearance before these same jurors, and even her lawyer, Jack Yocom, and his partner, Bill Wendt, wouldn't be allowed to speak inside the grand jury room, although they could consult with her and would eventually be furnished with a transcript of the questions.

During Sara's previous appearance before the grand jury, Tim McCormick had denounced her as a liar again and again. At times, he shouted, "All you do is lie!" It didn't seem to matter at all to McCormick that Sara had passed a police polygraph way back when the investigation started.

In fact, her story had never wavered. Sara continued to contend that her stepfather had come home, and then both had left on separate errands. Then they had returned and never left the house. She was certain she would have heard the loud muffler on his truck, or the sound of the truck rolling over the cattle guard outside their house, if he had gone out. Sara was certain that her stepfather was home from at least 9:30 P.M. until the following morning when both got up to ride to work together. Sara worked at the Carnahan family business in Nixa.

That story put Carnahan at home with Sara at the time police believed that Jackie was raped and beaten to death.

While Gerry Carnahan had refused a polygraph, Sara hadn't hesitated—and she had passed. What more could they want from her?

But her story couldn't be the truth, McCormick had insisted. He shouted "Liar!" again and again when she was on the stand and accused her of having fooled the polygraph. Sara's story had to be false, he said, because other witnesses had placed Carnahan in his old Chevy pickup right alongside and to the rear of the 7-11, when Jackie had popped in to buy hair spray and cigarettes. Carnahan must be lying when he said he was home with Sara. And why would he lie if he wasn't the killer?

Wearing round, wire-rimmed glasses and bearing a studious demeanor, McCormick, his red hair almost to his shoulders, appeared no more threatening than your average college professor—until he began to speak. Then he seemed to transform into an accusatory monster. Now, in the grand jury room, he gestured to the stand, and, from the previous times she had testified, Sara must have realized what was coming.

While Sara raised her right hand and was sworn in, McCormick stood in front of her, close enough that if she leaned over the railing of the witness stand she could probably touch him. The questioning, revealed in court records later made public, started quietly, and then moved to familiar territory. The accusations. The threats. "Have you ever seen the inside of a jail, Sara?"

She answered, "No, I've never been arrested," and then said firmly, "I'm a college student, not a criminal."

"Have you ever thought about what it would be like to spend the next few years in a penitentiary?"

She didn't answer.

McCormick was calm, his tone even. He was insistent but not loud, at least for a while, and then the accusations flew. "Liar!" he shouted.

Sara doggedly stuck to her original story. She and her stepfather had gone to the Repair Shop in Springfield the Monday night that Jackie was last seen. This was a restaurant that served alcohol. She was too young to legally drink so she ordered pop. Carnahan drank a few beers. They both ate tacos. They were with friends from work who would remember them, and she and Carnahan did not sit together.

Then both of them returned in Sara's yellow Volvo to the farmhouse on South National Road in Springfield. Her mother, Pat Collins, was away at a conference. Later, Sara went out to K-Mart to find a curling iron, but she was unable to find just the right one.

Jackie Johns had worked at K-Mart part-time, and Sara and Jackie knew each other from the brief time Jackie had worked at Garnett Carnahan's company, Springfield Aluminum, where Sara was currently employed. Although the girls were friendly, they didn't really hang out together.

Sara patiently repeated her story. She had returned home from K-Mart to find Gerry Carnahan in front of the TV. This time, however, she omitted mentioning that she knew he had stopped at the Vara Warehouse while she was out looking for a curling iron. She did say that he did not appear drunk or agitated.

The two of them had watched television, the first part of *The Tonight Show Starring Johnny Carson*, she testified. That started at 10 P.M. Central Time. Then both of them went to their separate beds. If Carnahan left after that, Sara told the jurors, she didn't hear the loud sound of his tires rolling across the tubes of the cattle guard near their house, which, because she was a light sleeper, would have awakened her.

McCormick turned his back on her. Then he wheeled.

"Gerry Carnahan is the one that murdered your friend, Jackie, and everybody knows it, and you are continuing to sit there and lie?"

Sara didn't move or answer. She didn't cringe. Like her stepfather had done with McNiel, she just maintained eye contact with McCormick.

"You are continuing to sit there and make it harder on yourself than it needs to be. All you have to do is tell us straight what you know."

"I am," she said.

McCormick was silent. He shuffled notes he held in his hands.

"Are you afraid he is going to do to you what he did to Jackie?"

And then, without waiting for an answer, he demanded, "Why are you covering for him? Why are you lying to these people?"

He kept firing the accusations like bullets.

"You told a different story in September."

"Why don't you get your story straight?"

"Do you know what you are saying?"

"You are lying for Gerry Carnahan and you are not even telling the same lies that he is."

"Sara, we have proof that you are in here lying to this grand jury. We know it."

"Nobody else is backing up your story. Gerry Carnahan has gotten you to lie for him."

"Sara, all the witnesses make a liar of you."

"Sara, I really feel sorry for you. You have come before this grand jury lying to try to cover it up and you are going to have to live with the consequences. I hope you sleep really well at night."

"I don't even know what is going on between the two of you."

"Nothing," Sara said at that point. "He's my step-father. That's all."

When it was finally over, she headed for the stairs. Reporters tried to stop her but she ignored them. When she got to where Shirley and Les had been, she hurried down the rest of the stairs. Her body language screamed, "I don't know anything! Leave me alone! I'm not a liar!"

But the grand jury believed otherwise. Shortly, they would indict Sara for felony perjury.

CHAPTER 13

MY BROTHER'S KEEPER

It was a hell of a way to spend a Saturday night, Kenny Carnahan thought, as he marched up the stairs leading to the office of Sheriff Dwight McNiel. Gerry Carnahan's brother had wanted to take his wife out to dinner, he would tell police, but the sheriff had summoned him for an interrogation that, Kenny admitted many years later, he feared would lead to a question he didn't want to answer: Why had he waited so long to tell what he knew about his brother's activities the night Jackie Johns was murdered?

The easy answer was because none of the army of cops investigating the murder had asked him. Perhaps the investigators had been gun-shy about talking to him because his brother Gerry, the prime suspect, had lawyered up back in June when he was first questioned. At that time, the family had hired the local legendary attorney Jack Yocom, who advised them to say nothing to any investigator unless he was present.

Now, it was January 18, 1986, seven months after Jackie's death and five days before his brother Gerry Carnahan would be indicted on evidence tampering and be forced again to go through a very public arrest and be reprocessed at the sheriff's department in Springfield and again in Christian County where he underwent a humiliating body search.

At 5:45 P.M., when Kenny arrived, it was already dark. He knew it didn't matter to Sheriff McNiel that it was a Saturday, because he'd told Kenny he didn't care one bit about his weekend plans.

Kenny realized that something unusual had to be up because he had again been required to appear that morning before a special Christian County grand jury. It had been impaneled five weeks earlier to solve the mystery of who had killed Jackie Johns. Kenny had lost count of how many times he had already been called before the grand jury, but he estimated it had to have been at least five. Sometimes Tim McCormick, the county prosecutor, had merely shouted at him for a while and then sent him out in the hallway to sit and think about whether he was telling the truth. It was humiliating, and certainly no way to treat a grown man.

In fact, the police had shown up so often at Kenny's door asking questions about Gerry that he and his wife had even considered moving to another part of the state. But Kenny had a good job at his father's factory and decided it was worth staying put, just for the job security.

Though he was three years younger than Kenny, Gerry had always been the favored son, the heir apparent to the Springfield Aluminum dynasty built by their father, Garnett. While Gerry worked in the office as a white-collar employee, Kenny worked in the factory.

Kenny realized that what he had been forced to tell the grand jury under oath that morning could hurt his brother. But because the sheriff had not been present, he now had to also tell him in person what he had said to the grand jurors. He was a family man, married with three children, and if he didn't cooperate, he could be thrown in jail for obstruction, especially if a judge granted him immunity from prosecution for anything connected to events in any way related to the murder of Jackie Johns.

When he got to the third floor, McNiel was waiting, his sidearm on his belt. A court stenographer was already sitting at her steno machine and smiled reassuringly at him.

McNiel waved him toward a chair. "Hello, Kenny. Thanks for coming in."

Kenny nodded.

"Just relax," McNiel suggested. "We won't be long."

It started off with the usual routine questions. Kenny acknowledged that yes, he was the thirty-one-year-old older brother of Gerald Carnahan, and that they both worked at the family's business, Springfield Aluminum, where Kenny was a "products structure developer" and Gerry was higher up the corporate ladder, working on developing bids and doing "research and development."

McNiel's demeanor was professional, firm, and civil. There was no browbeating and no leveling of threats. But Kenny remained apprehensive. Twice, he had been reminded to speak up so the court reporter could hear him. Soon, McNiel would get around to asking him why he had waited for seven long months to tell police what he had seen the night of June 17, 1985.

McNiel continued questioning Kenny slowly and methodically until he arrived at the night in question, when Jackie was last seen. "So what happened that night, Kenny?" the sheriff asked, his voice deceptively calm.

Kenny told him he had spent part of the night of June 17 with his parents and a number of relatives and friends in Branson, a forty-five-minute drive south of Nixa, at a country-western comedy called The Baldknobbers Show. Kenny said he'd driven the family's new white Cadillac on the return trip while his father, Garnett, and step-mother, Barbara, rode with others.

"Okay. So it would have been between 11:15 and 11:30 when you left Branson traveling north with this Cadillac, right?" McNiel asked, leading him to the obvious answer.

"Yes, sir. Between 11:15 and 11:45. Um, I don't remember exactly."

"Did you take that car directly to your home that night?"

"No, I went back to Garnett and Barbara's house."

"Were you going to drop the car off there?" McNiel prompted him.

"Yes, sir."

"Was someone following you there to pick you up?"

"No, sir."

"Well then, how were you going to get home?"

"In my truck," explained Kenny.

McNiel's questions continued to chip away at his witness's resistance, and slowly they zeroed in on the truth. Kenny had dropped off the Caddy at his parents' home, picked up his own truck, along with his wife and kids, and headed back up the side road labeled "CC," the same road that intersected with Highway 160 near the 7-11.

Just before that intersection, and only about two hundred yards kitty-corner from the spot where Jackie's Camaro would be found, Kenny said he had seen his brother's old pickup parked on the west side of the road. It was empty.

And in response to another question from McNiel, he admitted that yes, he had commented to his wife, "Is that Gerry's truck?"

"Okay," McNiel continued, drawing Kenny out, "so when your car pulled up to that intersection of the rural country road and the highway, you saw what you believed to be Gerry's truck sitting there. Is that right?"

"Yes, sir."

But the next day, when Kenny ran into his brother at the Springfield Aluminum plant, Carnahan insisted that it couldn't have been his truck because he had been home watching television with his stepdaughter, Sara. Also, Kenny said that weeks later, his brother stopped him at work and told him that if anyone, especially the police, asked if Kenny had seen anything, he was not to mention having seen Carnahan's pickup parked on CC that night.

Finally, as the questioning wore on, McNiel focused on a meeting that took place sometime in the fall of 1985. It was shortly before he'd received the warrant for Carnahan's arrest for evidence tampering, which he had used to arrest Gerry Carnahan at the Los Angeles airport.

"Did he tell you," asked McNiel, "that he felt pressured and that he wanted to leave before the grand jury issued a charge? To the best of your recollection, is that what he said?"

"Yes, sir," Kenny answered. He admitted to being appalled by that statement and said, "I turned around and walked out of his office."

And last but not least, McNiel asked Kenny why he hadn't mentioned all this earlier.

But Kenny Carnahan didn't really have an answer to that. He just shook his head and kept quiet. He was Gerry's older brother, but older wasn't necessarily stronger. Kenny had always known when to keep his mouth shut when it came to Gerry Carnahan.

The questioning ended about ten minutes later, and later that night, Kenny Carnahan drove to his home in Nixa. He knew Gerald was on a leave of absence from the family business and wasn't sure where his brother had gone. But that was fine with him.

Five days later, on Thursday, January 23, 1986, Kenny was watching the evening television when the announcer reported, "This just in! The police have arrested Gerald Carnahan in connection with the murder of Jackie Johns!"

Then, the camera flashed to a scene out on Highway 160 that showed his brother leaning over the hood of McNiel's cruiser as Sergeant Tom Martin watched soberly.

The reporter continued, explaining that Gerald Carnahan had just been indicted for evidence tampering, and although he had been free on $75,000 bail since early November for that same charge, the indictment required that he again be arrested, fingerprinted, and have new mug shots taken.

Kenny was stunned, as much by the presence of the TV crews at the scene as he was by his brother's arrest. Flipping through the stations, he saw the story on every single news report.

He shook his head. It sure looked like Sheriff McNiel had tipped off the stations. But as he would later say in court, he told himself, at this point, he could no longer be his brother's keeper.

CHAPTER 14

JACK

Jack Yocom, the veteran Missouri defense attorney, strode up the aisle between rows of pew-like seats in the Civil War–era Lafayette County Courthouse on December 9, 1986.

Court had not yet started and the judge was still in his chambers.

"How can this be tampering with evidence?" he questioned no one in particular, but he spoke loud enough so his opponent, Christian County prosecutor Tim McCormick, could hear. Yocom had been hired to defend Gerry Carnahan on his indictment for evidence tampering. McCormick ignored him.

Yocom wore a lemon yellow sports jacket and a maroon tie. His tortoiseshell glasses were, as usual, perched halfway down his nose, and his graying, receding hair was patted down neatly. When he strode into the courtroom, all eyes turned toward him. He had mastered the art of making a grand entrance, a skill many lawyers never learn.

McCormick, who had called Sara Collins a liar at least a hundred times before a grand jury, had been imported for the case, which had been moved to Lafayette County after a change of venue request was granted. No judge back in Christian County, where the indictment originated, could hope to find an unbiased jury when the defendant's name was Gerry Carnahan.

McCormick's red hair and beard made him stand out in the somber, oak-lined courtroom. He was a short, thin man in his late thirties who resembled a leprechaun. Now, he glared from a document-covered table ten feet from where Yocom was calmly perusing papers.

Circuit Judge Clifford Crouch was on the phone in his chambers. The jury was sequestered in the jury room, where a coffeepot had been set up beside a tray of jelly doughnuts. The seats in the old courtroom were nearly packed with residents of Nixa, present to support Jackie's parents.

Shirley and Les Johns staked out a seat in the front row and kept their eyes on Jack Yocom. They were desperate to convict Gerry Carnahan of something, anything. McCormick was under the most intense pressure imaginable to convict Carnahan of even a relatively minor felony. The public was convinced that Carnahan had murdered Jackie Johns, and they wanted his blood—for anything, at this point. If he did a few years in prison for evidence tampering, maybe investigators could use the time to dig in and finally make a murder charge stick against him. Just get him behind bars where he couldn't hurt any more young girls was the prevailing opinion.

So far, there wasn't near enough evidence for a murder charge, so evidence tampering would have to do. This wasn't a murder trial; far from it. But it was the only prosecution involving their daughter's murder, and Les looked confident of a win. Shirley, as usual, was inscrutable.

The judge and lawyers involved, however, knew there was an irrevocable line between a suspect who merely said he "didn't do it" and evidence tampering. In the United States, every accused person has a legal right to tell one lie in court: All defendants are allowed to plead not guilty even if they are as guilty as sin.

Yocom knew that if tampering could be construed as merely saying you didn't commit a crime when you actually did, then every defendant convicted at trial since the Constitution was ratified could be guilty of tampering.

He also knew that McCormick would produce a microcassette recording of Carnahan's interview with Sheriff Dwight McNiel and Springfield detective Rodney Burk. Yocom knew the story well. Carnahan had said that after he came home from a bar called the Repair Shop with his stepdaughter, Sara, both had left on separate errands before returning in time to listen to Johnny Carson's monologue at 10 P.M.

According to Carnahan, he never left the house again that night. Yocom expected McCormick to thrust the microcassette toward the jury box and insist that it was physical evidence. And if Carnahan lied about where he was that night, and if McCormick could produce enough witnesses to convince the jury that he had lied, then that was tampering because the words on the recording would be untrue.

But as Yocom loved to say, that argument was "a dog that wouldn't hunt."

Yocom sat down and opened his briefcase. He glanced over at McCormick and couldn't resist an opening, if unofficial, salvo. "If I can't hold it in my hand, or throw it on the floor, or toss it across the room or even see it, how can I tamper with it? Tamper with what? Tell me that, Tim."

Yocom, if his vast reputation as a grassroots, down-to-earth lawyer who couldn't resist using common words in court was any guide, probably figured his most powerful weapon was common sense. That's how he would defend Gerry Carnahan. All he'd have to do was assure jurors that evidence, to be tampered with, must actually exist in tangible form. Carnahan wasn't accused of breaking into the sheriff's office and somehow changing the words on the stenographer's statement. Instead, he was accused of making a statement that the sheriff claimed couldn't be true.

A statement was words. Words were like vapor. To call uttering false words "tampering," well, that would require a metaphysical outlook, Yocom insisted. It just wouldn't play in Lafayette County.

Yocom was already looking forward to the end of the trial; he would stand before the jury box, right up against the rail just feet away from the twelve good citizens of Lafayette County. He would slowly scan their faces and watch for any juror who turned away or did not appear to be paying attention. Then he would stand before that juror or jurors and bore in with the inescapable truth— that his client, Gerald Carnahan, could not be guilty of tampering with evidence *that did not exist.*

He would thrust his right arm up in the air, like a boxer. He had done it before during other memorable courtroom battles. His fist would be closed. The jurors' faces would show surprise, maybe even shock. Then, as he had said during a courtroom deposition months earlier concerning evidence in the tampering case, all he would have to do to convince a jury that Gerry Carnahan's denial about where he was on the night Jackie disappeared wasn't a crime would be to simply open his fist to reveal an empty hand. Depositions, where witnesses are sworn to tell the truth, are often held before a criminal or even a civil trial so that both sides in a case will not be surprised by unfamiliar testimony; a much different tack than the surprise questions Perry Mason used on the old television court drama.

"Can you see it?" That's what Yocom had asked Sheriff Dwight McNiel during the deposition concerning the so-called evidence that was supposedly tampered with. And McNiel had answered that he could see the tape cassette. But Yocom had countered by asking McNiel if the cassette had ever been outside of the custody of the sheriff's department, and McNiel had answered that it had not. And he had finally asked McNiel, if the cassette had never been outside the custody of the sheriff's department, how could Gerry Carnahan have tampered with it? McNiel said he didn't know.

Now, months later in the courthouse in Lafayette County, Yocom would ask Sheriff McNiel, who had been subpoenaed for the trial, the same question, but this time it would be in front of a jury.

If Yocom pulled it off, his fellow lawyers would undoubtedly get a big kick out of repeating the story when they gathered for cocktails at the annual bar association dinner in Springfield. They would all talk about how Jack Yocom had won that crazy evidence-tampering case.

Judge Clifford Crouch came in and called court into session. The first of forty scheduled witnesses was Detective Rodney Burk of the Springfield Police Department, but he testified without the jury present. Judge Crouch was concerned about the tampering charge and wanted to discuss whether the law even applied to Carnahan, but not with the jurors present.

Yocom provided Crouch and McCormick with a copy of a Missouri Court of Appeals decision made earlier that year. The crux of that decision, which went to the defense, referred to one sentence in the state's statute regarding tampering with evidence. It said a person is guilty of this crime when he "makes, presents or uses any record, document or thing knowing it to be false with the purpose to mislead a public servant who is or may be engaged in any official proceeding or investigation."

"Record, document or thing, Judge," Yocom said,

standing at the defense table. "We don't have anything like that here."

"Mr. McCormick?" Crouch asked, turning to the prosecutor.

Yocom sat down. McCormick stepped up close to the witness box. He held up a large envelope marked "Prosecutor's Exhibit 1."

Burk showed no emotion. "Detective, what is this?"

"It's a tape recorder cassette of a statement taken from Mr. Carnahan back in June of last year when we asked him about Jackie Johns and whether he had been at the 7-11 in Nixa that night."

"Is that your mark? The mark you used to place this into evidence?"

"It is."

"Your Honor?" McCormick said. "May I give this to the witness?"

Crouch nodded, and McCormick handed the envelope to Burk.

"You can touch it? Right?" McCormick said.

"Yes," Burk said.

"You can hold it. You can feel it. You can put it in a tape recorder and you can play it. Is that true?"

"Yes, it is."

But Yocom was ready on cross-examination.

"Detective, did Gerald Carnahan ever have access to that cassette?" Yocom asked.

"He did not."

"Has he ever touched it?"

"Not that I know of."

"Has it always been in the chain of custody? Have you always known where it is?"

"Yes."

"And where was it before you brought it here today?" Yocom continued, heading toward his concluding remarks.

"It was locked in the evidence vault at the police department in Springfield."

"Did Gerald Carnahan have a key to that evidence vault?"

"I'm sure he did not."

Yocom sensed then that he would never get the chance to make his argument before the jury. There was no way around it—Gerry Carnahan could not tamper with a cassette locked away in a police station. By introducing the cassette into the legal argument, McCormick had made a fatal mistake.

Yocom would have to be satisfied with just winning.

By focusing the argument on a tangible object, the prosecution had doomed itself. Yocom swung around in his chair and scanned the seated crowd of onlookers. He knew the jury would never be called.

He looked over at his client Gerry Carnahan and his wife, Pat Collins, at the back of the courtroom where they could make a quick exit. He had advised them that they should be ready to leave quickly. One of Yocom's associates had heard a rumor just after the hearing started that if Carnahan were acquitted, a sniper would be there to take a shot at him and his wife. Now, police were on guard outside the courthouse to prevent such an occurrence.

Yocom thought it was a good thing they were standing right beside the back door, ready to take off as soon as Crouch tossed the charge. They could avoid the horde of reporters who would lag behind to talk to him after Judge Crouch made his decision. And, based on his extensive court experience including dozens of decisions before that very same judge, Yocom had to be certain of what was about to happen.

"Your Honor," he spoke up. "I ask for this case to be dismissed because the law simply does not apply."

McCormick jumped to his feet. "Judge, this is the evidence. This is all that you need," he shouted as he held up the envelope containing the microcassette.

At this point, the judge called a recess and went to his chambers. He opened law books and eased back in a recliner while he read and read. But it was clear that the recent appeals court decision applied. Carnahan could not have tampered with evidence he had never had access to.

Court was reconvened and Crouch took the bench.

"This is a most difficult decision," he began.

Les Johns began shaking his head. Shirley Johns clenched her fists, and Jackie's three sisters looked stricken. Judge Crouch carefully explained the appeals court ruling and then, to no one's surprise, banged his gavel and said, "This leaves me no choice. Case dismissed."

Gerry Carnahan and his wife hurried to the parking lot and made their getaway in a Cadillac, while reporters crowded around Yocom and Sheriff Dwight McNiel as he left the courthouse on his way to the parking lot.

"Sheriff, is this the end of the Jackie Johns case?" a reporter shouted.

McNiel stopped and faced the reporters.

"Hell no, it's not over," he said. "And I have nothing else to say."

CHAPTER 15

THE TARGET

"Daddy, Daddy, you're on the TV," shouted thirteen-year-old Heather McNiel.

Dwight McNiel hurried into the living room, his nerves already on edge after Judge Crouch's ruling.

"Look," Heather said, pointing at the television set.

There on the six o'clock news, McNiel, to his shock and anger, saw close-ups of several human silhouette paper targets. The camera zoomed in on the name scrawled right at the top of each target. Bullet holes had penetrated some of the writing. But it was clear to McNiel's young daughter and to him that the name was "Dwight McNiel."

Her Daddy.

The image stayed on the television screen while the television reporter discussed what it meant. The targets, each pocked with bullet holes, were set against an earthen berm at a farm where right-wing extremist Glennon Paul Sweet had been captured just hours earlier hiding in an attic. A Highway Patrol SWAT team had arrested Sweet for the murder of Highway Patrol trooper Russell Harper, forty-five, who had been killed the previous day, February 8, 1987.

To McNiel, Harper's death was a tragedy for lawmen across the state, and he grieved for the trooper's family. But he was shocked and angry when the on-air reporters stated that Sweet had sworn to "get the sheriff," and that the investigating officers at the farm had let the media get so close to the targets. Hadn't they realized his kids would see their father's name on television, scrawled on a target by an extremist madman? Well, now the damage was done. He didn't know whether to just switch the channel or lead his daughter into another room. Heather looked at him in fear and confusion.

"It's nothing honey, nothing," he said. "Don't worry. That man will never be able to hurt us. Not where he's going." Sweet had finally gotten nailed for something that would eventually cost him his life in Missouri's execution chamber.

The reason that Sweet had considered McNiel his archenemy dated back more than two years, when McNiel, then chief deputy in Christian County, had humiliated Sweet in open court. Arrested on a drunk driving charge, Sweet had turned his "White Power" T-shirt inside out just before he was about to go to court. McNiel told him to turn it back around and Sweet refused. McNiel told him he would be turning it back around one way or the other so that the judge would know exactly who he was dealing with. Sweet simply laughed at him.

But that was how it went down in Judge Sam Appleby's courtroom at the Christian County courthouse. McNiel mentioned to the judge that Sweet was wearing apparel that made an interesting statement, and the judge saw that the defendant's shirt was inside out and suggested he turn it back around.

Sweet turned his shirt right side out, his resentment simmering. When he took his shirt off, court personnel saw that not only was the shirt offensive, but Sweet himself was covered in tattoos of swastikas on top of swastikas. Standing over six feet and weighing more than two hundred pounds, Sweet belonged to one of the most feared extremist groups in the county, "The Order."

But he had obeyed the court, and it was a humiliation he would never forget. And he knew it was McNiel who'd been behind it.

After he was released, Sweet sent word back to the sheriff's department through drug users who snitched to the cops. He told them that McNiel was going to pay for the insult one day.

Now, McNiel put his arm around his daughter's shoulder. This was one of the worst aspects of his job; having his innocent child exposed to the ugly underbelly of her dad's role as sheriff. Knowing her, he anticipated that she would begin dreaming about those targets with her father's name on them. But what McNiel had yet to fully realize, what he had ignored in his exuberance to change the world, was that the work of being a sheriff in one of the most violent areas of southwest Missouri was psychologically, as well as physically, dangerous.

Now, it was attacking his mental well-being. The violent death of a lawman he had known well began taking a toll that he would not be aware of until it was too late.

And then there was the matter of Gerry Carnahan. The pressure from Les and Shirley Johns to nail Carnahan for Jackie's murder had increased to the point that whenever they saw him, they turned their backs and told mutual acquaintances that McNiel "isn't the man for the job."

Jerry Estes from the Sale Barn Café joined in condemning McNiel as a bumbler. The town wanted Gerry Carnahan "strung up by his balls." Sheriff McNiel was all in favor of doing just that and more, but he and Tim McCormick, the prosecutor, had tried to nail Carnahan with the tampering charge, and it had backfired. There simply wasn't enough for a murder charge.

Shirley Johns had driven behind Carnahan's van one day on the outskirts of Nixa, shouting "murderer" out the window, or so Dwight had heard. There was a Springfield police report that Les and Shirley had parked one night outside Carnahan's house on South National Road with a loaded twelve-gauge pump shotgun lying between them on the transmission hump of their pickup. There was no charge and no violence that night.

But McNiel had gotten the message. If he couldn't do the job right, someone else would.

He couldn't blame them. Their daughter had been pulled out of her car, raped, and beaten to death with a bumper jack. These were terrible thoughts that would stay with them until the day they died. McNiel knew that even in their sleep, Les and Shirley could not escape imagining what Jackie must have gone through. They were constantly reminded of it by the continuous television and newspaper coverage, mostly focusing on Gerry Carnahan.

And what had McNiel provided? Nothing. In the photos taken when he was arrested on the tampering charge, Carnahan still had that faint smile on his face, and he was cocky on camera. He also wore the best suits and looked more like a lawyer than a suspect.

McNiel had hopes that the Sara Collins perjury trial set for April of that year would go his way. But that was about all he had going in the Jackie Johns murder case. If Sara Collins was convicted, however, it could be enough. The thought of going to jail even for a day for lying about her stepfather might motivate her to finally tell the truth about that night, McNiel theorized. If he could shake her testimony, and combine it with that of the other witnesses who swore they saw Carnahan that same night Jackie was last seen alive, there might be enough to charge him with murder.

Kenny Carnahan's statement that he saw his brother's distinctive pickup parked on Route CC at around the time Jackie was last seen was putting them closer to making an arrest. Between that and the witnesses who had seen Carnahan and his truck behind the 7-11, McNiel was tempted to push McCormick and the local judge for a murder warrant and take a long shot that a jury might convict.

But if they didn't, there would not be a second chance.

On the last day of testimony in the Collins perjury case, April 27, 1987, Debbie Sue Lewis of Willard went missing. It had been a frustrating 1986 for Sheriff Dwight McNiel, whose investigation of the murder of Jackie Johns had been virtually stalled for lack of evidence against his prime suspect Gerry Carnahan. And no other likely suspect had emerged.

Lewis's disappearance was a missing persons case, handled by the Greene County Sheriff's Department. Because McNiel was to the south in another county, he was not initially informed. But had he been told of the circumstances around the thirty-one-year-old woman's disappearance—that her car was found on Highway 160 with the door open and her purse still in the front seat— he would have had a lot to contribute.

CHAPTER 16

DEBBIE SUE

Reporter B. J. Honicutt drove toward the small town of Willard, Missouri, on his way home after ten hours of chasing crime and car crashes for radio station KGBX in Springfield. He worked a general assignment beat, which meant he covered anything his editor threw his way. He was good-natured, always a plus when working a beat that requires rapport with police. And he never became irritated when people asked "B. J. Honicutt, like the M.A.S.H guy?" That B. J. was a Hunnicutt not a Honicutt, he would patiently point out.

It was nearly 11:30 P.M. on Monday, April 27, 1987, a clear, cool night. All day he had been jumping from story to story. Earlier in his shift, he had been keeping tabs on the close of the Sara Collins perjury trial, still a big story locally because of listener interest that persisted from the Jackie Johns murder headlines two years before.

Sara Collins was accused of lying to a grand jury to protect Gerry Carnahan, her stepfather. Although she had initially insisted that he had come home sometime before 10 P.M. the night Jackie disappeared, and that he never left again, her story had changed. When pressed before a grand jury she later said that he *had* left the house to go to the Vara Warehouse while she was at K-Mart. This shift in testimony had cast serious doubt on her story.

Testimony had finished at the courthouse in Forsyth, down in Taney County, where Collins's trial had been moved. It was a "bench trial," held before a judge who would decide the verdict, instead of a jury. That had been Collins's choice; she believed her chances were better with one judge, rather than nine jurors.

Honicutt broadcasted a fifteen-second update on the trial based on notes he had made from phone calls to court sources. He hadn't had time to drive the fifty miles to Taney County to cover it live. The testimony in the trial had now ended, and the judge announced he would take several days before he would give his verdict.

Honicutt had the radio tuned to his own station as he drove north along Illinois 160, the same Missouri highway where Jackie Johns's abandoned Camaro had been found twenty miles or so to the south in June of 1985.

Up ahead on the left, on the shoulder of the oncoming lane, he spotted a Volkswagen with the driver's door open. Only the parking lights were on. He stopped and took a long look, but didn't get out of his own car. The car was under a streetlamp, and the artificial light made it hard to be sure of the VW's color. Maybe it was a light shade of yellow. But he was sure it was an early 1970s model.

It appeared to Honicutt that someone had run into car trouble, but it puzzled him that the driver's door had been left open. He looked up and down the road, but saw nothing else suspicious.

Honicutt drove on until he spotted a Willard police officer parked in a supermarket lot, and told him about the abandoned car. Then, feeling his civic duty done, Honicutt drove home.

Two days later, he was at the radio station in Springfield when he got a call from the Greene County Sheriff's Department. A deputy asked if he knew a Debbie Sue Lewis. She was thirty-one years old, five feet three inches, and about 105 pounds. She had long, brown straight hair and preferred cowboy boots and hats.

Honicutt was told that Debbie Sue was missing, and her VW—the car Honicutt had reported to the cop—had been impounded.

The VW was registered to Debbie Sue, but she hadn't shown up at her apartment in Walnut Grove. The police had found the driver's door open and her purse, containing cash, lying on the front passenger seat. The parking lights were on and the keys were in the ignition. But there was no sign of Debbie Sue.

Investigators for the Greene County Sheriff's Department under Sheriff John Pierpont were responsible for locating her because the spot where her VW was found was just outside the Willard city limits.

Honicutt didn't know Debbie Sue Lewis. But his reporter instincts told him that there was probably a story in there involving that seemingly abandoned VW. He wanted to know more about who Debbie was and where she might have gone.

He learned that thirty-one-year-old Debbie Sue was considered a carefree soul, always ready for an adventure. At least that's what her friends told police. Honicutt's source said investigators theorized she might simply have met someone she wanted to spend time with. But leaving her car on the highway with the door open and her purse inside was strange indeed. Honicutt knew that could only mean that something bad must have happened.

His source said Greene County deputies were investigating a report of an argument between Debbie Sue and two still-unidentified men at a north Springfield bar a few hours before Honicutt had spotted her car. Years later, after he had moved on from the news business, Honicutt clearly remembered details from the night he found the Volkswagen. "I thought, 'Maybe I should check out that bar,'" he said, "'and see if there's enough information for a story.'"

He also found out from another source that just minutes before he'd spotted Debbie Sue's car, a deputy sheriff also on his way home after work saw a car pulled off the road with the hood up. But as he was about to stop, the deputy saw a light-colored VW pull in behind the car. Figuring that the driver of the disabled car had called a friend or relative for help, the deputy continued on his way home.

It didn't take long for Honicutt to realize he had heard a story like this before, or at least parts of it. He recalled that Jackie Johns's Camaro had also been found with the driver's door open, twenty-five miles away on the same highway. He also recalled that Jackie's keys and purse had, like Debbie Sue's, been found in her car.

"I think I was just a few minutes behind an abduction," he told his editor. "And it's the weirdest feeling."

———

The day after Debbie Sue's car was found, her parents, Elmer and Marie Lewis, were grilling hamburgers and watching the sun go down when a security van at the Cloud 9 Ranch Club in West Plains in Missouri's Ozarks pulled up at the camping spot for their Winnebago. They were told to immediately call the Greene County Sheriff's Department back in Springfield where the retired couple lived.

Elmer made the call and was told that on the previous night, his daughter's car had been found abandoned on the highway near her home outside Willard. Elmer and his wife needed to pack up and return home immediately.

Frantic, the older couple left their Winnebago with friends and drove their car back to Springfield. The two-hour drive seemed endless, and both of them were sick with fear as the miles ticked by.

"Don't worry, she'll be OK. There must be an explanation to this," Elmer told his wife. Marie folded her shaking hands in her lap and nervously looked out the window. She said little on the drive back home.

"It'll be OK," he reassured her again. But he didn't believe it. As he recalled years later, he knew something ugly had happened to his daughter.

They drove directly to the sheriff's department, where they heard the theory that their daughter had pulled behind a still-unidentified car with its hood up. They were shown Debbie Sue's purse and keys, which they quickly identified as hers. They had checked her apartment. She had never shown up. None of her neighbors had seen her since earlier in the day before.

Elmer sat beside his wife at a table in an interrogation room, his arm around her shoulder. Now, it was their turn to talk. The investigators wanted to know all about Debbie Sue.

Elmer did the talking, explaining that his daughter worked as a licensed practical nurse for a Springfield cancer specialist. Formerly, she had worked at St. John's Hospital in Springfield and knew many people on its staff. She loved horses and rodeo events and often wore a cowboy hat and boots. She did not have a steady boyfriend, as far as her parents knew, but she often dated.

She loved horses so much, added Elmer, that she had once been allowed to drive a team of the Budweiser Clydesdales that had visited Springfield from the brewery's headquarters in St. Louis.

But as for enemies, Elmer couldn't think of a single person.

"Marie? What about that? Did your daughter know anyone who had fought or argued with her? Anything like that? A former boyfriend maybe?" a detective asked.

Marie shook her head and burst into tears.

"No, we don't know of anyone like that," Elmer said. "She got along with everybody. I don't know anyone who would want to do her any harm."

Two weeks later, Elmer and Marie Lewis watched Sundance, Debbie Sue's big Irish setter, as the dog lay in the sun in their backyard. They had taken the dog in as their own. There had been no word of Debbie Sue: It was as if she had decided to walk away from her car and her life and never return.

But that scenario made no sense. Debbie Sue had never done anything like that before. She had seemed happy. And most important, she would never just walk out on her "baby," Sundance. Suddenly, as Elmer watched, Sundance picked up his head and barked. Then he leaped up and ran for the street, barking all the way.

Elmer followed, unsure what had alarmed the dog. Marie watched from a window and then came outside.

A neighbor, a woman about Debbie Sue's age, had pulled up in front of the house. Like Debbie Sue, she also drove a 1970s VW. Sundance ran to the driver's door, tail wagging a mile a minute. Then he backed away, his tail drooped, and he retreated to the sidewalk where he lay down and put his chin on the cement. Elmer knelt down and gently patted the dog's head.

"It's not Debbie," he said soothingly. "It's not Debbie Sue. But she'll be coming home. You wait and see. She'll be back. She hasn't forgotten us."

A few days later, Elmer Lewis stood at the top of a small, treeless hill within sight of the tiny community of Walnut Grove. It was a hot, hazy afternoon in May 1987. Using binoculars, he could easily make out the duplex a mile away where his thirty-one-year-old daughter, Debbie Sue, had lived before she disappeared more than two weeks earlier under very disturbing circumstances.

Elmer was seventy years old and retired. He and a friend had climbed the hill on a surreal mission; they intended to watch for vultures that might be circling above his dead daughter's body. It had seemed like such an insane thing to do. But a cop had actually suggested it. The Greene County Sheriff's Department detective assigned to his daughter's missing person case had sent him on this grim mission. Elmer had been told to sit on a high point near his daughter's home and scan the sky for circling buzzards. Maybe the birds would lead him to her dead body. His friend had tried to talk him out of going, saying people would think Elmer wasn't right in the head if he traipsed across the prairie in search of a revolting bird feasting on his daughter's carrion.

"I don't need to hear talk like that. She's not dead," Elmer had said.

Another cop, a friend of many years, told him that because her car was found with the driver's door open and her purse still on the front seat with money in it, chances were good that Debbie Sue was dead. Of course, that only made Elmer feel worse. But his daughter had vanished and he had to help her. He just couldn't sit around the house and do nothing.

After Debbie Sue vanished, the orderly life he and his wife, Marie, had carved out for themselves became so frightening and confused that Elmer sometimes forgot where he was and what he was doing.

But not today.

Now, he lowered the binoculars. He knew he should be home with Marie but he had to do this.

"This is crazy," Elmer said to his friend. "You were right. They should have a task force or something doing this kind of thing." He scanned the sky. Turkey buzzards, a type of vulture, are common in Missouri, but he couldn't spot even one.

But as he sat in the hot sun, Elmer realized that something was wrong about the way the case was being investigated. Very wrong. How many other fathers whose daughters had gone missing were asked to perch on a hill and look for buzzards that might be consuming their child's dead body?

A short week later, Elmer was sent on another mission. The detective had called his home in Springfield and requested that he obtain his daughter's dental records.

When Elmer uttered, "Oh, my God," the detective had quickly said, "Oh, it's just a precaution, in case we find her." He got the records and delivered them to the sheriff's department.

The detective then asked him to go to the department's motor pool garage to examine the exterior of his daughter's 1974 Volkswagen. It had been found on Highway 160 about 11 P.M. on the night of April 27, within a mile of her apartment.

Elmer Lewis again did as he was asked and carefully examined the car. The only thing he found notable was a large dent on the passenger-side rear fender. The deputies thanked him, but they refused to give him any information about their investigation and would not let him look inside the car.

"What about that big dent?" he asked.

"It's under investigation," they told him.

About a month later, Elmer got another call from the sheriff's department. The detective on his daughter's case had been replaced. Later that day, he learned from his longtime cop friend that the previous detective, the one who had sent him up the hill to watch for buzzards, had left the sheriff's department.

The new investigator was an older man who focused on a lead from the night that Debbie Sue was last seen. It put her at a north Springfield sports bar where two men had accosted her in the parking lot. Onlookers had said one of the men had tried to push his way into her Volkswagen, but she had managed to drive off without him.

The detective learned their identities and traced the men to Neosho in Newton County in the far southwestern corner of Missouri. Once there, he questioned them both, but each insisted he knew nothing about what had happened to Debbie Sue after she left the bar. The men had criminal records for drugs, but the detective found

Murder on a Lonely Road   141

nothing more to tie them to the Volkswagen on that night.

And then, when Elmer Lewis still had hope that the persistent, older detective might find his daughter, the man retired.

When he learned of the detective's retirement, Elmer told his wife Marie, "The bottom has dropped out. There's nothing going on. I don't know what we can do."

There was a small reward for information about Debbie Sue Lewis based on donations totaling about $3,000. Flyers with her photo had been posted around Springfield and throughout the few blocks that made up Walnut Grove.

Elmer had driven up and down the roads looking for anything that might be connected to his daughter. Each night he had returned to Marie, dejected. Yet each morning when he got up, he planned his entire day around searching for Debbie Sue.

One night he and Marie remembered that during the previous summer Debbie Sue had talked about a guy she and her girlfriends had met at Table Rock Lake. The guy, who called himself "Gerry," had shown up in a speedboat when the boat they'd been using to water-ski broke down and had offered to tow them.

Debbie Sue later saw this same "Gerry" on television during a report on the murder of Jackie Johns of Nixa. During the report, a photograph of a man named "Gerald Carnahan" had been shown. Elmer and Marie recalled Debbie Sue excitedly telling them that this was the same "Gerry" she'd met at the lake.

Elmer Lewis had also heard Carnahan's name mentioned by some of the deputies when he had gone to the garage to examine his daughter's car. He'd heard them talk about the similarity between Jackie's disappearance and Debbie Sue's. But he hadn't paid much attention. There were always a lot of rumors going around.

But after he got to thinking about it and talking more with his wife, Elmer went to the main branch of the Springfield-Greene County Library District and learned to use the microfiche machine. He looked up everything he could find printed in the *News-Leader* about Carnahan.

From his research, he learned that Gerald Carnahan was an avid volleyball player and participated in a league at the Ozark Mountain Stadium in Springfield. That was where Debbie Sue worked part-time at night pushing a cart that offered soft drinks and hot dogs.

"She could have gotten to know him. I'm saying it could have happened," he told Marie.

And there were the obvious similarities to the disappearance of Jackie Johns two years earlier. Jackie's Camaro had been found on the same road—Highway 160. Like Debbie Sue's Volkswagen, the Camaro was found on the side of a highway, driver's door ajar, keys in the ignition and her purse on the front seat.

But the Volkswagen had not been splattered with blood.

Elmer didn't know what to think. He doubted that his daughter would have dated a man like Carnahan if she knew he was suspected of murdering a young woman.

"But Gerry didn't walk around with a sign on his neck that said, 'Murder suspect,'" Elmer told friends.

And then in October 1987, Elmer and Marie received hope that their daughter was still alive. It came in a report to police from a Kansas man on his way home from Orlando, Florida. He'd been passing through Springfield and happened to spot one of the fliers showing Debbie Sue as a missing person.

The man called the Greene County Sheriff's Department and said he was certain that back in Orlando he had dated a woman who matched the photo in the flier. Hoping this was a solid lead, Sheriff John Pierpont told reporters that his investigators had contacted police in Florida. They had agreed to question people in a neighborhood described by the man from Kansas.

"This is the first real lead that we've had," Pierpont said during a press conference at the sheriff's department.

Elmer and Marie prayed that Debbie Sue would call or even write and let them know she was alive. They would immediately forgive her for running off and leading them to believe she had been murdered.

A television reporter interviewed Elmer Lewis about his missing daughter, and he had looked straight into the camera and said, "Debbie Sue, just come home. Our arms will be open for you."

Hope returned to the family. Sundance still whined and ran to the curb whenever a car pulled up driven by a young woman, though when the big Irish setter realized it wasn't Debbie Sue, he would turn away and hide in the backyard.

Marie, who had been ill with something thought to be the flu, began to recover and the couple started going out to see friends again. They believed Debbie Sue would be coming home eventually. She just needed time to sort things out.

But a week later, word came from police that a woman who looked enough like Debbie Sue to be her twin had been located near Orlando and questioned. It was the same person who had dated the man from Kansas.

But it wasn't Debbie Sue.

CHAPTER 17

CHRISTMAS TREE

In the forests of Missouri's central Ozarks in December of 1987, the ground was barren. The frozen, muted landscape was a haven to whitetail deer, cottontail rabbits, and fat, yellow-bellied fox squirrels, nearly invisible against the browns and grays.

On December 10, David Wood and his wife walked the snowless acres of their wooded property in a remote part of Newton County near Joplin, searching for a Christmas tree. It was a few minutes after noon on a cloudy day, and they had just parked their pickup truck along WPA Road, which dead-ended not far from their farmhouse.

Wood had walked only about seventy-five feet into the woods when he spotted something pink and white on the ground among the fallen leaves up ahead. He walked to the spot and stopped, noticing what first looked like a turquoise-colored rag. He saw that it was lying next to what looked like light blue gym shorts with a floral pattern.

Then he realized that the gym shorts were around a human pelvic bone. For a moment he stood motionless, not sure that he was seeing right. Were these human remains lying right in front of him? Then he spotted a hand protruding from a jacket.

"Oh, my God!" he yelled to his wife. "Meet me at the truck, quick!" Minutes later, after arriving back at their house, Wood called the dispatcher at the Newton County Sheriff's Department and described the remains found on WPA Road.

Newton County chief deputy Ron Doerge was at the sheriff's office in Joplin when a call came in from patrol. A man and his wife had found human skeletal remains not far from the road, and Doerge was needed immediately to take over the investigation.

On the short drive to the site, Doerge, who rode alone, got another radio call. A coonhound owned by another resident of WPA Road had just come trotting home with a human skull in its teeth.

"What the hell is going on?" Doerge wondered. Grabbing the cruiser's microphone, he said, "Repeat that?"

"This is four one," came the response. Doerge recognized the call sign of Deputy Bob Butterfield.

"A hunting dog found somebody's skull out on WPA Road or somewhere around there. The homeowner's got it," Butterfield said. "I can go get it."

Human remains in the woods and a skull-fetching

hound? Well, why not? Doerge knew that WPA Road had been used as a body dump before.

His deputy, Randy Watson, waited at the edge of the road with other officers. Doerge could see that less than one hundred feet into the woods, yellow police crime scene barrier tape had been strung from tree to tree, protecting a circular area about thirty feet across.

"What have we got now?" Doerge asked.

"I would say it's a homicide, but things are kind of scattered. C'mon, I'll show you," Watson said.

Deputy Preston Koelling was already photographing what, at first glance, looked like colorful rags scattered among the leaves and overgrown vines.

Doerge ordered Watson to contact pathologist Dr. Phillip Whittle, who worked for the county coroner, and get him out to the woods as quickly as possible. Then he ducked under the crime scene tape for a closer look, careful where he stepped.

He saw the white and pink tennis shoes, with the foot bones still in them. The laces were still tied, and multicolored striped socks still held foot bones. He knew that it would take a long time to shake that image from his memory.

The skeleton lay mostly within the barrier of tape, but had been pulled apart by animals and insects. A few small bones were found some distance away.

Doerge noticed the turquoise leg warmers, which extended to the ankles, still on the lower leg bones. On the pelvic bone was a pair of light blue shorts with a darker blue flower design. And easily visible in the space where the shorts drooped from the bone, he could see black bikini-style underwear.

Nearby was a red, blue, and green striped jacket with a white cotton lining. The arm bones were still inside the sleeves. There were no rings on the finger bones. There were also scraps of a white and pink blouse lying near the jacket.

On closer examination, Doerge and Watson saw thin nylon rope wrapped around some of the finger bones of the left hand. It was looped and knotted in such a way that led Doerge to believe the victim must have had her hands tied behind her back.

There was no skull in sight, but a large patch of brown hair was found, and wrapped around it was an elastic headband. A white plastic banana-style hair clip also turned up under leaves.

Vines had grown over some of the bones. It was clear that the remains had lain in the woods for months.

"What about the skull?" Doerge asked Watson.

"Butterfield's got it. Some loose teeth, too," Watson replied.

"That's some coonhound! A real cadaver dog," said Doerge.

"Yeah. It's the damndest thing."

At 4:30 P.M. they were finished. The nearly complete skeleton had been placed in a body bag and taken to the coroner's office in Joplin for autopsy. As for human remains, Dr. Whittle had found only bones, except for the large piece of hair still attached to leathery scalp tissue.

Whittle's initial report noted that the victim was female and probably not older than thirty to thirty-five. There were no obvious signs of trauma. He found no bullet holes or broken bones. The clothing, although it had deteriorated due to weather exposure, wasn't torn. The rope was used to tie the victim's hands, probably behind her back. The specific cause of death eluded Whittle, but the manner of death was definitely homicide.

Doerge served as his department's methamphetamine expert because the woods of Newton County were infested with meth cookers. His immediate suspicion was that this unfortunate woman was somehow connected to the extreme violence of the meth dealers.

There was a missing twenty-six-year-old woman named Ruth[1] from Seagoville, Texas, whom snitches said had been murdered in Newton County for bragging to friends about having watched a local drug dealer cook up a batch of meth. In an interview from several months earlier, a snitch known in the report only as "Carla" said that Ruth had fled the state and returned to Texas on a bus, only to turn around and come right back to Missouri to the home of a man called "Bill," who had previously beaten her. Bill, according to Newton County sheriff's intelligence reports, was a known meth dealer whom Carla, according to the report, said she'd heard brag about having gotten "rid of" Ruth.

---

1 Denotes pseudonym

The file on the woman also contained details about a former Newton County deputy who'd picked her up hitchhiking and dropped her off at a known meth dealer's house, according to an earlier sheriff's department investigative report. The dealer ended up being sent to federal prison, and Ruth wasn't seen again. The deputy had not been suspected of any crime. Doerge and Watson contacted Texas authorities for information, but nothing showed that Ruth had ever returned to her home state.

But Doerge and Watson doubted their skeleton was the girl from Texas. The missing Ruth was described on her driver's license as being five feet six inches and 155 pounds, while the bikini underwear found on the skeleton from WPA Road was clearly smaller. This victim was petite and probably didn't weigh much over 100 pounds.

Several hours later, Whittle finished his autopsy and confirmed that the victim could not have weighed more than 110 pounds and was about five feet two inches in height. However, the examination turned up little else, including cause of death, though Whittle said strangulation could not be ruled out. The tiny hyoid bone located in the throat, which could indicate whether the victim had been strangled, had not been recovered.

———

The next day, December 11, 1987, Deputy Warren Schmidt of the Greene County Sheriff's Department called. He had received a copy of the notice sent to all Missouri police departments describing the remains found off WPA Road, including a list of the clothing.

Schmidt told Doerge that, based on the clothing, he was sure the skeleton was Debbie Sue Lewis.

Several hours later, dental records confirmed the identity of the remains. It was indeed Debbie Sue Lewis. Her parents Elmer and Marie Lewis also identified the photos as showing their daughter's clothing.

Greene County's eight-month-old missing person case was officially confirmed as a homicide. But the official investigation stayed in Newton County, since that was where Debbie Sue's remains were found.

All the available information, which was limited to the autopsy, was transferred to the sheriff's department in Greene County. And as he helped transfer the details of the autopsy and the discovery of Debbie Sue's remains to the far more populous county up north, Doerge heard talk of a name he would never forget. It was "Gerald L. Carnahan," the prime suspect in the murder of Jackie Johns. He had heard the name before from newspaper and television reports, but he hadn't paid much attention. Newton County had enough problems. He didn't need to be looking at cases from other counties.

Unless of course, as he would come to believe, the deaths of Jackie Johns and Debbie Sue Lewis were connected.

The Greene County investigators told Doerge that a witness put Carnahan at a bar in Springfield, where Lewis had been seen on the night she disappeared. And there was information from another witness and from the victim's family that she might have previously met Gerry Carnahan.

Doerge, who would go on to become sheriff in Newton County and lead a local war on methamphetamine makers, never forgot Gerry Carnahan.

"I guess they got a suspect," he recalled Deputy Watson said.

"Yeah, don't you know about that guy?" Doerge said he told Watson. "That boy has got some reputation. Damn! We sure don't need him messing around down here. We've got enough trouble as it is!"

Top Left: Jacquelin Sue (Jackie) Johns in her 1983 Nixa High School senior class yearbook photo. NIXA PUBLIC SCHOOLS YEARBOOK

Above Right: Lisa Fitzpatrick, left, and Jackie Johns wear formal gowns for their 1983 senior prom. DAYNA SPENCER

Left to right: Dayna Spencer, Lisa Fitzpatrick, and Jackie Johns in 1984. The best friends all lived in the small town of Nixa, Missouri, several miles south of Springfield. DAYNA SPENCER

Dayna Spencer, left, and Jackie Johns. After Jackie's murder in 1985, Spencer became a police officer. DAYNA SPENCER

Jackie Johns's coffin at her wake in Nixa High School in June 1985. Because the funeral director anticipated that her many friends and admirers would want to attend, the wake was held in the school's gymnasium. Several hundred people showed up to pay their respects. DAYNA SPENCER

Dayna Spencer at Jackie Johns's grave near Nixa, Missouri. Jackie's mother, Shirley Johns, was later buried beside her daughter. GEORGE PAWLACZYK

Top Left: Dwight McNiel in 1985 during his first year as the elected sheriff of Christian County, Missouri. The thirty-two-year-old McNiel helped lead the initial investigation into the rape and murder of twenty-year-old Jackie Johns. J. DWIGHT McNIEL

Above Right: Christian County Sheriff Dwight McNiel vowed that Gerald Carnahan would eventually be arrested and successfully prosecuted for the rape and murder of Jackie Johns. But McNiel was forced to wait over twenty years before a DNA match led to Carnahan's conviction. J. DWIGHT McNIEL

Police mug shot of Gerald Carnahan on the day of his arrest in Missouri in November 1985 after he was returned from Los Angeles, charged with evidence tampering for allegedly lying to police about his whereabouts on the night Jackie Johns disappeared. The charge was later dismissed.
CHRISTIAN COUNTY SHERIFF'S DEPARTMENT

Gerald Carnahan and his wife, Pat Collins, in the law library at the Greene County courthouse in Springfield, Missouri, prior to the start of a bail hearing on July 30, 1993. Carnahan, who faced trial on an attempted kidnapping charge, was already free on bond on two earlier counts including arson. Over a prosecutor's objection, his bond was continued. *SPRINGFIELD NEWS-LEADER*

Debbie Sue Lewis in the backyard of her parents' home in Springfield, Missouri, with her dog, Sundance. In April 1987, eight months after she went missing, her skeletal remains were found in a remote wooded area in southwestern Missouri. Ruled a homicide, her death was never solved, though Gerald Carnahan was a suspect. ELMER LEWIS

MISSING

SHERRILL LEVITT
AGE 47, 5'0", 110 POUNDS, BROWN EYES, BLONDE COLLAR - LENGTH WAVY HAIR, THIN BUILD, LAST SEEN WEARING FLOWERED DRESS

SUZIE STREETER
AGE 19, 5'5", 102 POUNDS, BROWN EYES, BLONDE STRAIGHT HAIR, BIRTHMARK ON RIGHT CHIN AND ON RIGHT ARM, LAST SEEN WEARING BLUE JEANS, WHITE T-SHIRT & PINK SHOES

STACY McCALL
AGE 18, 5'3", 120 POUNDS, BLUE EYES, BLONDE BELOW-SHOULDER STRAIGHT HAIR, LAST SEEN WEARING FLOWERED SHORTS, YELLOW T-SHIRT & BROWN SANDLES

Call SPRINGFIELD POLICE DEPARTMENT
(417) 864-1700

REWARD FUND ESTABLISHED Call Missouri Victim Center For Information 863-7273

Police also suspected that Carnahan was involved in the baffling 1992 disappearance of two girls and a mother from a home in Springfield on the night the two young women graduated from high school. However, no evidence was ever developed linking Carnahan to the women. Their fate remains unknown. SPRINGFIELD POLICE DEPARTMENT

Former Christian County Sheriff Dwight McNiel created this unique dart board with Carnahan as the bull's-eye to help him focus on his vow of bringing the rich boy businessman to justice for the rape and murder of Jackie Johns. GEORGE PAWLACZYK

Gerald Carnahan, forty-nine, escorted into a Greene County, Missouri, courtroom following his arrest on August 9, 2007 for the forcible rape and murder of local beauty queen Jackie Johns in 1985. He was denied bail and held for trial. SPRINGFIELD NEWS-LEADER

Left: Missouri State Highway Patrol Sergeant Dan Nash, a professional climbing guide in his off-duty time, sent a vaginal swab for testing that would break open the long-stalled Jackie Johns murder case. It led to Carnahan's arrest in August 2007. DAN NASH

Right: Jason Wyckoff, a criminalist and supervisor of DNA testing at the Missouri State Highway Patrol forensic lab in Jefferson City, whose testing of the semen evidence in the Jackie Johns case led to a quadrillions to one match to Gerald Carnahan. GEORGE PAWLACZYK

Left: Springfield defense attorney Dee Wampler, who survived a bout with cancer that delayed the Gerald Carnahan murder trial, vigorously challenged the DNA evidence that pointed to his client. DEE WAMPLER

Right: Assistant prosecutor Casey Clark of the Greene County prosecutor's office handled crucial questioning in the Carnahan case. Two days after the September 23, 2010 guilty verdict, Clark married his fiancée. CASEY CLARK

CHAPTER 18

THE NAIL

In late September 1988, Sheriff Dwight McNiel sat in a bar, contemplating ordering another drink, when he felt a hand on his shoulder and looked up. As McNiel would later recall, it was Bruce Harris, his good friend and fellow member of Christian County's own unofficial political powerhouse, the "Scotch/Irish Syndicate." For McNiel, the events that would ensue over the next several years and would dramatically affect his life picked up speed that night with an important political decision. He would remember these times in exact detail.

Harris sat down on a barstool next to his friend. The place was nearly empty, and McNiel offered a wan grin and ordered two bottles of Bud.

Harris was dying of cancer but never let it affect his outlook. He was always steady, always a friend, and he sensed that his buddy, Dwight, was having increased doubts about being sheriff. It was time to talk politics, even though the next election was more than a year away. Harris, the elected county circuit clerk, was a pretty fair politician and had helped McNiel destroy Buff Lamb three years earlier in the 1984 Republican primary and defeat the Democratic candidate for sheriff in 1984. Harris, McNiel, and prosecutor Tim McCormick had gone door-to-door, passing out campaign literature announcing that it was time for a change, and Dwight McNiel was the ball of fire the town needed for sheriff.

But that night, Dwight McNiel hardly looked like an energetic ball of fire. Instead, he doodled on a piece of paper set on the bar. "Look at this," he said to Harris. "We've got him. Check this out."

McNiel drew a square that he labeled "7-11." Then he drew an "X" at one end of the square.

"That's Gerry right there, in his damn truck," he said, stabbing at the X. "We've got three witnesses who say he was right behind the 7-11. And his own brother Ken puts his truck right here on CC, see, right here!"

He drew a "T" and labeled the long end "160" and the short end "CC." Then, he drew another "X" at a point on the straight line labeled "160."

"This is her car on 160, right there at this X. All he had to do was leave her car there on the highway and just cut across a field for maybe two hundred yards and he's right back at his truck on CC. Witnesses swear to all of this. And yet the son of a bitch walks free. He backs out of his polygraph, gets a big money lawyer, and we can't lay a hand on him."

Harris nodded. He'd heard it all before.

"You'll get him," Harris told his friend, "and he knows you'll get him. He's gonna trip up."

"Yeah, well we're not even close," McNiel admitted, his tone dropping to a low murmur.

Actually, at that very moment, McNiel wasn't even sure where Gerald Carnahan was. He had heard that Gerry might be in Taiwan on a business trip. Or maybe South America.

From interviews he had conducted with Detective Rod Burk of the Springfield Police Department, McNiel knew that Carnahan had plenty of contacts in South America, too. There were countries down there where Nazis had hidden out for decades. Why not Carnahan? He could flee to Uruguay or even to Chile or Argentina and no one would ever find him.

Many years later, McNiel would talk at length about what it meant to pursue Gerry Carnahan and fail to turn up enough to slap handcuffs on him for Jackie's murder; how it would eat at him until he began to doubt his own abilities. It was times like having a beer in that Ozark bar that he never forgot, when a good friend was there to counsel him.

"What's really bothering you?" McNiel remembered his friend as saying. And he would never forget his own answer.

"Hell, I'll tell you. It's this. My family can't go to the Wal-Mart or to church without people staring at them because I'm standing right there and I'm the guy who can't catch Gerry," he said. "My family is taking it on the chin because of me. I'm the one letting Jackie's murderer live the high life. I'm the one letting him get away. But if I knew of any damned way to get something to pin him to her death, I'd do it. But there's nothing. Nothing that would hold up in court."

"There's more bothering you than Gerry." Harris nudged his friend. "Come on, what's going on with you?"

But McNiel did not want to unload his personal problems on a friend who had only recently been told he had untreatable cancer and had only a short time to live. Harris was just forty-four and had a wife and kids. How could he tell him that the thick binders on his desk back at the sheriff's department, the ones holding more than 150 transcribed witness interviews, mocked him? That he couldn't stand to look at them? That they reminded him that he'd failed in his grand mission to change the world when he'd arrived at the sheriff's department?

How could he admit that his first major case, the Jackie Johns murder, was rapidly heading to the cold case shelf? Did he want to do this for the best years of his life? Didn't his family deserve more?

The binders contained enough information to write an encyclopedia on the life of Jackie Johns and had taken months to accumulate. But there wasn't one solid clue in the thousands of pages that could lead to an arrest. If he had been able to arrest Carnahan, McNiel thought, Debbie Sue Lewis might not have been snatched out of her car and murdered. Gerry Carnahan was now the prime suspect in that case, too, and that murder investigation was going nowhere, either.

In Newton County, where Debbie Sue's skeleton had been found, the small sheriff's department could not carry out a massive investigation like the one Christian County and the Springfield Police Department had conducted in Jackie's murder. Well, didn't Debbie Sue deserve justice, too?

But the possible links to Carnahan, although they were real enough, fell far short of justifying an arrest warrant in Debbie Sue's case as well. Sure, there was evidence that they knew each other and that they'd probably met at Table Rock Lake, when Carnahan had offered to use his boat to pull Debbie and her friends on their water skis. There was even a witness who thought she'd seen Carnahan at the same bar where Debbie Sue had been spotted a few hours before her abandoned car was found.

And his failure to solve the Jackie Johns case had caused such bad feelings that he couldn't even approach the Johns family, who used to be his friends.

Shirley Johns had died that past February, and Les Johns said his wife had "grieved herself to death" over the loss of their daughter. Now, Les wouldn't even speak to McNiel. He blamed him for his daughter's murderer getting away scot-free and urged his friends not to support McNiel if he ran again for sheriff.

At the Sale Barn Café, Jerry Estes, too, had turned his back on McNiel for the same reason. Like Les Johns, Estes told friends he had no doubt that Carnahan had killed Jackie, even though neither of them had any real evidence.

It wasn't just the Gerald Carnahan case that made McNiel question whether he had chosen the right path by becoming sheriff. He also felt that the deaths of the troopers and the unfathomable violence of the white extremists who used Missouri as their home territory were almost beyond his ability to overcome.

In his nightmares, McNiel still saw the bloody bodies of Troopers Jimmie Linegar and Russell Harper sprawled on the pavement. There had been nothing anyone could do for them. But whenever he or one of his deputies stopped an old pickup truck or a suspicious vehicle, a crazed member of a local extremist hate group might pop up with an automatic weapon and start firing. Christian County had become a dumping ground for corpses of combatants in the furious local gun battles to control the methamphetamine market.

"It used to be like Mayberry here," he told Harris. "Now it's become Chicago."

At age thirty-five, Dwight McNiel was beginning to gray prematurely. For the first time in his life he began to question why he had ever wanted to be sheriff.

Now, coming back to the present, he told his friend that he didn't want to bother Harris with his problems.

"You're not bothering me," Harris said. "But maybe you ought to think about walking away. Just walk away from it. You've done all you can for Jackie. Somebody will get Gerry one way or the other."

A week later, McNiel made his decision. He wouldn't run. Instead, he decided to buy a Ford dealership and sell cars. The idea had come from a friend who had sup-

ported him politically and owned a dealership. He said
he would help McNiel, and that owners of dealerships
had a big influence in county politics. Dwight McNiel
could still be a player, just in a different way.

He could also still help with the hunt for evidence to
nail Gerry Carnahan; after all, he'd always be a trained
investigator. Selling cars might even leave him enough
spare time to push his own investigation. The way things
were at the sheriff's department, he could barely keep up
with the paperwork involved with the drug murders that
kept popping up.

Dwight McNiel took pride in the fact that he left the
sheriff's department a better place than when he took
over that first insane day. The evidence room had been
restored. The Jackie Johns material occupied an entire
shelf. Even more voluminous records on her case were
kept at the Springfield Police Department. And he had
seen to it that his department's communication system
was modernized.

As for himself, he was confident that he could land on
his feet even after all the psychological blows he'd been
dealt, but he would be sorely tested on that score. As it
turned out, McNiel didn't get his dealership—he was
outbid. For a while, he sold used cars on a small lot in
Ozark. He sat behind a desk with customers' low-score
credit reports, trying to find a way to convince a bank
that they deserved a loan. But that job dribbled away in
time. For the first time in his adult life, he found himself
with time on his hands and without a steady paycheck.

His marriage began falling apart, and he worried

about the effect on his four children. At this point it seemed that the world was changing in ways he would never have predicted. He was now thirty-seven years old and unemployed. The Jackie Johns case, which was the case he most cared about, the one that would forever be associated with him, was a shambles. And now his home life was at risk.

Soon afterward, his wife, Susan, asked for a divorce and McNiel did the honorable thing: He moved out. The court documents from the divorce showed he turned over all assets to his wife and assumed all the couple's debt. His lawyer asked him if he was crazy, and McNiel replied that he didn't know for sure. Even the divorce court judge asked if he had thought out this decision.

"It's my idea, Your Honor," McNiel had emphasized. He was going to do right by his family, no matter what the sacrifice was to his own security.

Before he was entirely aware of what was happening, McNiel was nearly bankrupt. He owned a faded white 1977 Chevrolet Impala, his clothes and tools, and a semiautomatic 9 mm pistol. He owned no property and kept no bank account. He called a man he had once arrested who, despite convictions for theft, had become a friend. This unlikely friend owned a few rental properties in Ozark, including a one-room walk-up with the bathroom located down the hall. This became "McNiel & Associates," a private investigation firm—only there were no associates. There was no telephone, either; only a bed, a beat-up dresser, and a cheap fan.

And there was a mirror. McNiel took a long look at

himself and saw a man who had sunk lower than he had ever gone in his life.

At night, he sat on the edge of his bed and thought about Gerry Carnahan. Could he really be blamed because Carnahan had not been arrested? Could he be blamed that Carnahan had beaten the evidence-tampering charge? Was it his fault that Sara Collins had been found not guilty on the perjury charge? Was it all because McNiel couldn't handle the pressure?

Bruce Harris had looked cancer in the eye and hadn't folded, but Dwight McNiel felt he'd let the pressure get the best of him.

Many years later, comfortable in his success as one of Missouri's top private eyes, McNiel was asked if this had been the worst time in his life. He said it was and went one better, saying he could remember exactly what he once told a bartender down the street from his walk-up, one-room temporary digs: "Sometimes you're the hammer. And sometimes, you're the nail. Today, I feel like the nail."

CHAPTER 19

THREE MISSING WOMEN

On June 6, 1992, eighteen-year-old Suzanne Streeter and nineteen-year-old Stacy McCall graduated from Kickapoo High School in Springfield, Missouri.

By the morning of June 7, both girls and Suzanne's mother, forty-seven-year-old Sherrill Levitt, had vanished.

By June 8, residents of Springfield began realizing what had really happened. And when they did, they could talk of nothing else.

All three women had disappeared from the same house on the same night. Their three cars were parked outside. Their purses were lined up on a stairway. There was no sign of a struggle, and a Yorkshire terrier named Cinnamon appeared to be the only witness.

The day after they vanished, the *News-Leader* used its biggest type for a front-page headline, "No Trace," which could be read a hundred feet away. Below it were photos of the three: Sherrill Levitt; her daughter, Suzanne Streeter; and Suzanne's best friend, Stacy McCall.

When family and friends first reported them missing on Sunday, June 7, police had not appeared concerned. An officer left a card on Sherrill Levitt's front door with a note to call headquarters. They expected that the women would show up soon.

But by June 8, panic set in and a record thirty detectives were assigned to the case.

This was what was known:

On the night of June 6, Suzanne and Stacy had attended their graduation at Kickapoo High School. Sherrill had watched the ceremony and then went back home. The young women had partied with friends and other graduates, then scrapped plans to stay at another friend's house and drive to the resort town of Branson for breakfast.

Instead, after attending several graduation parties, Suzanne told Stacy to follow her back home to her house. They were thought to have arrived after midnight.

No money or personal items were missing from the women's purses or from the house. Both girls, heavy smokers, had left their precious cigarettes behind. And oddly, their purses were found neatly placed on stairs leading down to Sherrill Levitt's sunken bedroom. The television was on, but the picture was fuzzy. Sherrill had been on the phone at around 11:15 P.M., talking with a friend about repainting a chest of drawers. The friend told police that Sherrill sounded relaxed and happy. Police found her prescription glasses on a nightstand, along with a book placed facedown to mark the page. Her bed appeared to have been slept in.

Stacy McCall's shorts were found folded over her tennis shoes, leaving her frantic mother to believe someone had carried her daughter off in her underwear and a T-shirt.

Police never saw any evidence that violence might have occurred.

Janelle Kirby, a graduate who had partied with both of the young women, came over the next morning with her boyfriend when her phone calls went unanswered. When they found shards of a broken glass globe that covered the porch light on the front stoop, Janelle's boyfriend swept up the broken glass from the porch and threw it away, never guessing that it could be evidence.

By the time Springfield Police fully realized that a kidnapping—and probably much worse—had occurred, nearly twenty relatives and friends had already walked through the home, no doubt destroying key evidence.

———

At its peak, the media gave this story even more attention than Jackie Johns's murder seven years earlier. By this time, the Johns case had gone cold, although Gerald Carnahan was still considered the only suspect.

What went unnoticed in the crush of investigating the missing women those first days were the vague similarities to both Jackie's murder in 1985 and the disappearance and murder two years later of Debbie Sue Lewis. But no one was thinking that Carnahan could be involved in the Springfield case. Not yet.

Springfield Police were not inclined to link their crime to a long-cold case of murder in another town. And yet, there were similarities.

For instance, the broken light globe. In Jackie's Camaro the overhead light dome lens or cover was missing, but the bulb was intact. In both Jackie's and Debbie's murders, the victims' purses had been left untouched, even though they were in plain view and contained cash. On East Delmar Street, three purses were lined up ready to be pilfered yet went untouched.

And in both previous murders, the perpetrator left the victim's car and keys there for the taking.

In the disappearance, three cars were parked right outside with the keys in the purses.

It wasn't until several days later that one of Stacy's friends happened to mention to police that she had picked up the phone and heard an obscene call on the answering machine—but unfortunately, she had erased it. When asked why she had done that, she said she just thought she would be helping Sherrill and Suzanne, who she'd fully expected would show up that day. The police were unable to determine when the message had been left.

Janelle Kirby reported that a few days earlier she, too, had gotten such a call. In fact, as a *News-Leader* story mentioned, people all over the area had been receiving obscene calls since the early spring.

Investigators in Jackie's murder had also interviewed more than a dozen young women who claimed they had been receiving obscene phone calls during the spring and early summer of 1985. Jackie received some of those calls in the weeks before her murder. Even so, police did not see the calls as connected to her killer.

One oddity about the missing women case, which at first shocked and intensely interested investigators, was that Suzanne's ex-boyfriend was facing felony charges of grave robbing. He was accused of taking a skull from a mausoleum in Springfield, yanking out several teeth, and selling the gold fillings at a pawnshop for thirty dollars. It was a shocking crime, even though it was essentially only vandalism and theft.

But the young man passed a polygraph and was ruled out as a suspect in the disappearance.

During the ensuing days, undercover and uniformed officers searched the neighborhood house-by-house and backyard-by-backyard. They located a few witnesses who said they'd seen a blond woman with short hair who looked like Sherrill Levitt. They said she was driving an older-model, moss-colored Dodge van and appeared terrified. This would have been during the day on June 7.

The nonstop barrage of publicity about the missing women, both in print and on television and radio, resulted in hundreds of calls to the Springfield Police Department from citizens who thought they saw or heard something that might help the cops find the women. The entire city was on edge.

One man, who was shopping at a grocery store,

became suspicious when he saw a blond woman sitting behind the wheel of a similar-looking van. He even wrote the license number on a newspaper, but then threw it away. Under hypnosis, he remembered the first three numbers, but it didn't help. The cops still couldn't locate such a vehicle.

The television crime show *America's Most Wanted* profiled the case in late December 1992. A caller who seemed to have reliable information was disconnected before he could be put in touch with a Springfield police officer in the show's studio. Despite on-air pleas to call back, the man was never heard from again.

One suspect did make headlines. Robert Craig Cox, convicted of beating a woman to death in Florida and sentenced to death, had spent ten years on death row before getting released in 1988, when an appeals court ruled there hadn't been enough evidence to convict.

A former army paratrooper with boyish good looks, Cox taunted police, telling them he knew where Sherrill, Suzanne, and Stacy were buried. He was questioned about the missing women, but never arrested—at least not for that crime. Cox later ended up in Plano, Texas, where he took a young girl hostage while robbing a bank. He was caught and convicted, and his earliest parole wouldn't be until 2025.

It was Gerry Carnahan who would eventually inherit the mantle of the public's favorite "suspect" in the case of the three missing women.

By this time, seven long years had passed since Jackie Johns's remains had been found in Lake Springfield.

From time to time, the *Springfield News-Leader* and other local newspapers continued to publish stories about the crime, the number one unsolved homicide in southwestern Missouri. Jackie's father Les Johns was often interviewed and steadfastly urged investigators not to let the now cold case be forgotten.

It wasn't, nor was Gerry Carnahan.

As the Springfield case developed into what investigators came to conclude had to be a case of murder, the leap to associating the number one suspect in the Jackie case to this latest mystery was an easy one for the public to make, even without any evidence tying Carnahan to the disappearance. As a result, Jackie's familiar portrait began appearing on newspaper front pages along with the photos of the missing Springfield women in stories where local lawmen were quoted urging that Carnahan be questioned in this disappearance case. The only connection to Carnahan was a persistent rumor that Levitt had once cut his hair.

At the time of the women's disappearance, Carnahan and his wife, Pat, lived four miles due east of Sherrill Levitt's home on East Delmar. They had moved from their old farmhouse across from the golf course in Nixa to Springfield several years prior to South Devon Road in Springfield, though Carnahan remained director of research and development at Springfield Aluminum in Nixa. The Carnahan residence on South Devon was connected to East Delmar in a four-mile, straight-line drive by East Sunshine Street.

During that time, according to an order of protection

Pat Collins filed in November 1992 in a Christian County court, Carnahan was out of control. He was abusing several antidepressants and getting drunk every day. He had begun waving a pistol while he staggered around their home. He had attacked his wife with a hot iron. He had run over Pat's foot with his car. He vowed he wouldn't kill her because with a quick death she wouldn't suffer enough. He wished he could give her a sexually transmitted disease.

All these allegations were contained in the order of protection that Collins filed and then inexplicably asked the court to withdraw only two weeks later. But at the time she signed the order of protection, she swore to its truthfulness.

However, it wasn't until later that Gerry Carnahan would be publicly linked with the case that became known throughout the state as the "Three Missing Women." Officials would call for him to be investigated regarding the disappearance, but there was no evidence linking him to the crime. He was not brought before a judge. Police did not question him.

Instead, it was the public who conferred the title of "favorite suspect" upon him.

Carnahan's notoriety seemed to come naturally. He had the uncanny ability to convince the public that he was a true-life bogeyman, even though he looked like a well-dressed businessman.

Maybe it was the way he talked, or the way he walked, or all the trouble he would get into a few months later in 1993.

CHAPTER 20

IN THE HEADLIGHTS

Heather Starkey wanted out of her boyfriend's car—right away! It didn't matter that she would have to walk the rest of the way home at 2 A.M. on a chilly Saturday in March 1993.

She was so angry that when her boyfriend hit the brakes along Ingram Mill Road, she slapped his face and jumped out. Months later, she wouldn't remember exactly what had started the lingering argument hours earlier at a party at a friend's house in Springfield.

"We just didn't click," was all she would say when asked under oath.

Alone on the road, the slender eighteen-year-old high school senior hurried along the shoulder, intending to walk to a friend's house about five minutes away and get a ride home from there. She wore a green sweater, blue jeans, and low-cut boots. A thin layer of sleet made walking difficult, and Heather rubbed her arms to ward off the cold.

The area where she was let out was semirural, but Heather wasn't concerned for her safety. She saw a well-lighted Git-N-Go store on her side of the road just ahead and figured she could use a pay phone there to call her friend.

Few cars passed, but Heather was confident she would soon be home.

As she came up to the edge of the convenience store's parking lot, a new white Chrysler drove past her from behind and then stopped about fifty yards in front. The driver parked at a sharp angle, as if he intended to block her path. The car's headlights were left on, and Heather froze, unable to decide whether she should turn and run or stand her ground. She would well remember the details of the next few moments of horror when asked to recount them in a courtroom.

She watched as a man in his midthirties wearing an overcoat got out of the passenger side of the Chrysler and headed directly for her at a fast walk. He covered the ground so quickly that when she turned to flee, he was already within an arm's length. He said something like "Are you all right?"

Before she could react, he grabbed her arm and Heather screamed.

The man seemed to be pushing her toward woods about one hundred feet away but slipped on the sleet after they had gone less than ten feet and Heather fell with him. She twisted on the frozen ground, trying to pull herself free. Heather was horrified by her assailant's strength. Again, she screamed for help and flailed at him with her free arm.

Then, she managed to get her feet under her while he still held her arm in a viselike grip. This allowed her to use both legs to push upward with all her might. She broke free of his grasp and ran to the convenience store, sobbing and calling out for help.

Liz Zaagsma was in the passenger seat of her boyfriend's car as they drove south along Ingram Mill Road. As they approached the Git-N-Go she saw a struggle along the side of the road. A man lunged toward a young woman on the ground, and Zaagsma turned in her seat to keep the scene in view, not entirely sure what she had just seen.

Then she saw the girl get up and run toward the store. She knew then that she had just witnessed an attack of some sort. But the girl appeared to be safe, and Zaagsma saw the attacker get back into a white Chrysler driven by another man.

As she and her boyfriend continued south along Ingram Mill Road, the Chrysler came up close behind them and she could see the driver and his passenger.

Zaagsma got the plate number—QNX-377—and managed to find a pen to write it down on a scrap of paper. She nervously watched the other car, afraid that she and her boyfriend might be the next to be attacked. Finally, the Chrysler turned off on a side road.

When she got home, Zaagsma called the Springfield Police Department and reported the plate number to a dispatcher. Four days later, on Thursday, March 18, 1993, an arrest team made up of Christian County sheriff's deputies, Nixa Police, and a detective from the Springfield Police Department arrested Gerald Carnahan. He was picked up at his office at Springfield Aluminum.

Police had traced the license plate on the Chrysler to a rental car Gerry had been using while his own car was being repaired. Eric Turnage, who had been driving the rental car, was a friend of Gerry's. He said he'd had no idea what his friend had intended when he told him to pull over on the side of Ingram Mill Road. Turnage told police that while he saw Gerry walk toward Starkey, he was shocked when the two began struggling. He said when Gerry came back to the car, he asked what had happened but was told only that it was a misunderstanding.

Based on Heather Starkey's account to police and the license plate number from Liz Zaagsma, Gerry Carnahan was taken to the Greene County courthouse and charged with attempted kidnapping. He was released that afternoon after posting cash bail of $15,000 but faced a maximum of seven years in prison.

Once again, Gerry was front-page news. Now, the "bogeyman" was snatching young girls right off the street. Jackie Johns's photo also hit the news, as readers were reminded that Gerry was still the prime suspect in her death. But most people didn't need reminding, because Jackie Johns had not been forgotten.

CHAPTER 21

THE BOGEYMAN

It was a whopper of a story—Gerald Carnahan, the Ozark Bogeyman, was the most notorious bad guy to come along since Jesse James. He seemed untouchable. He even came from a rich family who bailed him out of jail whenever he needed it. Forty-four-year-old *Springfield News-Leader* city editor Lou Ziegler knew that readers hated rich boys who got away with crime more than sin itself. Readers would be glued to the papers and viewers to the TV to learn more about him.

Ziegler realized that if a town like Springfield had a genuine bogeyman that scared the crap out of people, that would be the story that sold newspapers. Ziegler, who was revered by his reporters—on any given day, he was feared, adored, and hated, sometimes all at once—couldn't turn the story over to just any reporter, and even a reliable beat reporter wouldn't do.

A monster like Gerry Carnahan required a special reporter. By the time he was charged with attempting to kidnap Heather Starkey, Carnahan had a hurricane-size notoriety, deserved or not. In addition to the Jackie Johns and Debbie Sue Lewis cases, the baffling disappearance of the three Springfield women the year before still fueled media attention, and Carnahan's name was often mentioned in connection to their case.

Ziegler needed a writer who would not cringe from or be overwhelmed by this infamy. He scanned the newsroom. There was only one choice. He picked up his phone and dialed Ron Davis's extension.

"Get in here," he told him. "I've got a story for you." It was Wednesday, March 17, 1993. On Saturday, March 13, Carnahan allegedly attempted to kidnap Heather Starkey.

Davis was the paper's top reporter and far and away its best writer with awards to prove it. And that meant he could take a few liberties with his appearance.

He wore his dark hair shoulder length, and his hairdresser put a purple streak on one side and a yellow streak on the other. She suggested wearing a spherical Japanese religious bell about twice the size of a marble tied way in the back of his coiffure. It would be an elegant touch, she said. Davis was thirty-two years old and ready for anything. He thought the bell was just what he needed.

The mission was simple. Get to know Gerry Carnahan better than any reporter. Get close to him, closer than anybody else. And don't let anyone beat you to the punch on any aspect of the story.

"You are going to get me the Gerry Carnahan story," Ziegler told Davis. "I don't want you to judge him. I want you to know him better than any other reporter. I want him to live and breathe on our front page. If he burps, I want to know what he burps, why he burps, and how it smells. He dragged a high school girl off the road, for Christ sake. Everybody in this city is going to read what you write."

Davis knew what he had to do before Ziegler even opened his mouth, but he kept quiet. His boss was a great editor who let him do pretty much as he pleased. Carnahan was the biggest story in town. Hell, he was the biggest story in the entire state.

Davis already knew Carnahan from covering events connected with Jackie Johns's death in 1985. He had even attended the "non-trial" when Judge Crouch threw out the evidence-tampering charge.

But that was before Carnahan's notoriety went viral.

Ziegler told Davis that he wanted a huge front-page story for the Saturday, March 20, 1993, edition. There would be a detailed graphic of the attempted kidnapping showing the exact positions taken by Carnahan and his alleged victim, and the rented Chrysler Carnahan's friend Eric Turnage had been driving.

Ziegler wanted Davis to interview Christian County sheriff Steve Whitney, who had held the job since McNiel left. Ziegler wanted to know if Whitney believed Carnahan was a killer, and he knew Davis could get him talking.

On Saturday morning, the *News-Leader*'s subscribers

read Davis's report splashed across the entire front page under the headline "Sheriff Links Suspect to Slaying."

As Ziegler expected, Whitney said he believed Gerry Carnahan had killed Jackie Johns. Other lawmen named in the story linked Carnahan to Debbie Sue Lewis, whose skeleton had been found in late 1987. Still other cops mentioned Carnahan in relation to the 1992 disappearance of the Springfield women: Sherrill Levitt; her daughter, Suzie Streeter; and Suzie's friend, Stacy McCall. The three were missing without a trace.

And there was Kelle Ann Workman, who'd last been seen alive on the evening of June 30, 1989, mowing grass in a cemetery in Oldfield in Christian County about fifteen miles southeast of Nixa. Her body was found in a creek bed a week later.

Kelle would have stood out as she mowed the grass on that extremely hot evening. She was only twenty-four, with strawberry blonde hair and an athletic build. She was just over six feet tall, a physical attribute that had served her well when she wore the blue and gold of the Ava High School girls' basketball team. Whatever happened on that sticky hot evening, it didn't involve Kelle's car, an older model Oldsmobile Cutlass, which was found nearby with the keys still in the ignition.

That small detail, the keys in the ignition, was also true in the Jackie Johns and Debbie Sue Lewis investigations. Kelle's car was found in the church driveway, and the church lawn mower was located close by in a parking lot. In the nearby cemetery, investigators saw that only about a third of the grass around the headstones had been mowed.

There was no sign of Kelle.

That very night, search parties combed the nearby woods and police officers scoured the myriad back roads in this primarily rural area. But they found nothing that would lead them to the missing woman.

On July 7, a farmer found the partially decomposed body of a woman in a dry creek bed in a section of the Mark Twain National Forest. Dental records confirmed that it was Kelle Ann Workman.

Because of decomposition, a cause of death could not be determined. However, given that the remains were found about nine miles from where Kelle had been cutting grass yet her car was left untouched, indicating that she may have been kidnapped, the manner of death was ruled a homicide. Pathologist Dr. John Overman's report stated that strangulation was a possibility and sexual assault could not be confirmed.

A rumor that the notorious Gerald Carnahan had been seen that very day at a convenience store in the small community of Dogwood, near where Kelle lived with her parents, fueled speculative reports in the media, and the public began to feel that Carnahan could kill at whim and never be caught.

Were these victims the handiwork of a serial killer? And was that serial killer Gerald Carnahan? If there was any evidence, cops weren't using it to get arrest warrants.

At Carnahan's arraignment on the attempted kidnapping, his lawyer, Jack Yocom, took his customary spot at center stage and told the horde of media that his client was unfairly tagged as a "bad guy."

"They've made a crusade over him. He's got a reputation as a real bad boy—completely unjustified under the circumstances," Yocom said.

But the media circus fired up several months later in November 1993. Judge Frank Conley was determined to try the case in Greene County, no matter what the public opinion of Gerry Carnahan. When jury selection started, newspaper and television reporters crowded around whenever Carnahan left the courtroom. At one point a television cameraman was backing up as he was shooting Carnahan and his entourage and smacked the back of his head into a telephone pole. It knocked him to the ground. Carnahan extended his arms likes Moses and commanded the throng, "Stop!" Then he knelt and asked the dazed cameraman if he was all right.

At the noon break in the jury selection, when the media milled around him, Gerry Carnahan turned to Ron Davis and said, "Want to go to lunch?"

"Hell, yeah," Davis said.

It worked, just as Ziegler knew it would. His reporter could ingratiate himself with almost anyone—even reputed serial killers. And Ziegler knew that Davis would not get too close to his subject. Davis would present the complete Carnahan, warts and all.

As Davis and Carnahan climbed into Carnahan's gold Cadillac, Davis couldn't resist waving to the other reporters as they pulled away. He even smiled. He was sitting next to the best interview around, Gerald Carnahan himself. That's what his boss Lou Ziegler had told him. Get close to Gerry. And Davis was doing just that. And in a Cadillac to boot.

They drove to the Crosstown Barbecue Restaurant on East Division Street and took a table in the center of the dining room. Moments later, Davis realized something was wrong. The busy place was silent. Carnahan looked up from his menu. And as Davis remembered and often retold, the other diners were silently staring at him as if he were holding a .44 Magnum. They knew who he was. He was Gerry Carnahan, the Ozark Bogeyman.

Carnahan growled, "What, d'ya see something green?"

The patrons quickly turned away and Carnahan ordered a steak, medium rare.

"Gerry Carnahan is a badass," Davis told Ziegler back in the newsroom. "I've never seen anybody stare him down."

"I don't care if he's the 'Man in the Moon,' " Ziegler said. "Just keep him on the front page."

That afternoon, County Judge Conley gave up trying to find impartial jurors who had never heard of Gerald Carnahan. On a motion filed by the defense, he ordered the trial moved 150 miles to Boone County. The courthouse was in Columbia, the university town and home of the University of Missouri, renowned for its school of journalism. Davis knew he'd be given travel money for a motel and meals.

He was on the road again. Life was good—and the story was going to be even better.

CHAPTER 22

THE INTRUDER

A few months before Gerry Carnahan's attempted kidnapping trial, sometime near midnight on Friday, September 17, 1993, an intruder had used a steel pry bar to try to force open an overhead loading door at the Custom Aluminum Foundry on West High Street in Aurora, a small town about thirty-five miles south of Nixa. The intruder left pry marks but couldn't get the door opened, and his footprints led away from the door. He'd made no attempt to conceal his footprints in the soft ground. The prints were deep and sharp edged, and could easily be identified as having been made by a large-size man's athletic shoe. Cheap brown cotton gloves were also left at the scene.

On the north side of a warehouse attached to the foundry the intruder found a second overhead loading dock door secured only by a padlock. A quick crunch with bolt cutters dropped the lock. He opened the door but was thwarted by a locked interior door. He left the bolt cutters on the loading dock.

For some reason, he sprayed red paint just below the window on the locked driver's side of a white Ford panel truck parked at the edge of the cement loading dock. Then he used a discarded metal hand pump to smash the driver's window. Bits of glass flew across the seats.

In the driver's seat, he jammed a screwdriver into the ignition, a crude but effective car thief's trick. But the truck's battery was so weak the engine barely turned over and would not start. The intruder dropped the screwdriver on the floor. Then, he left the truck and, still not caring about footprints, went to the shipping room door on the west side of the warehouse. He pried off the door handle and threw it into bushes.

He slipped inside the dark building, which was temporarily closed because of a lack of business. Streetlights would have allowed enough light for him to maneuver once inside.

In the men's restroom, he spilled black ink from a bottle he left in a sink and tried to clean the ink up with paper towels, but did a lousy job.

He found the production area of the foundry, a large room on the east side of the business that contained pallets loaded with very expensive sand molds used to cast various aluminum parts for fishing boats. Each cast weighed fifty pounds and was worth about $2,000. A fishing boat manufacturer had provided the casts. There were hundreds of them, stacked neatly on wood pallets.

The fishing boat company owned the casts, which were loaned to the foundry that made the actual boat parts from molten aluminum.

The man spent about an hour lugging dozens of the molds one by one to a vehicle he had parked near the foundry. Traffic would have been very sparse at this time of night. He actually wore a rut in the dirt carrying the loot.

Inside the foundry, the mud on his shoes again left clear imprints. He dropped one glove in the production room and another in a hallway. Once again, he sprayed red paint, this time about five feet up the wall on the west side of the production room. It was just a splotch, like a Rorschach ink blot. At some point, the intruder piled empty pallets near the north end of the production room just a few feet from the remaining and still-stacked sand cast molds he hadn't carried off. Using gasoline, he set the pallets ablaze and fled. It left a "V" burn pattern on the concrete floor, a dead giveaway that the fire had been intentionally set.

At 7 A.M. the next morning, just hours after the Aurora Fire Department put out the fire, Missouri state fire marshal Bill Farr arrived at the foundry. Trucks and men from the fire department were still at the scene. They had been there since responding to a call made by a passing motorist, who saw flames coming from the foundry just after midnight.

Randy Haycook, an investigator who worked for Farr, was already at the scene examining the damage.

"Whattya got, Randy?" Farr asked, handing him a

cup of coffee with two creams and two sugars. They had worked dozens of cases together, and his boss knew how Haycook took his coffee.

"It's a burglary and an incendiary fire," said Haycook. "Unusual stuff was taken, like sand molds. They use them to make boat parts. They're expensive as hell—I think something like a couple of grand apiece."

Like all trained fire investigators, Haycook avoided calling the blaze "arson," which actually referred to a fire set specifically for profit. In this case, it appeared clear that the perpetrator had set the fire in a botched attempt to destroy evidence of a theft. However, the fire did little more than char an area of the production room floor about the size of a kiddie swimming pool.

Haycook showed Farr the gloves and the areas where the ink had been spilled and where the red paint had been sprayed. The fire hadn't affected this vandalism or symbolism or whatever it was intended to be. Spilled ink. Red paint. Footprints. Bolt cutters left where they would easily be found.

It felt like a spur-of-the-moment theft that hadn't been well thought out—the work of an amateur.

As for the ink and paint, Farr knew that burglars often displayed inexplicable peculiarities at a crime scene, as if prowling around in the dark on someone else's property excited their darkest side. He knew that textbooks on the psychology of crime contained chapters detailing the weird acts of burglars who sometimes urinated or even defecated at a crime scene. Was this intended to be a message of some kind?

That's what some psychologists theorized. But Farr, like many professional investigators, simply thought such weirdness was evidence of nervousness.

"Does the owner know?" said Farr.

Haycook, who had been rousted out of sleep by the emergency dispatcher, flipped pages of his notebook.

"Wes and Delores Burt," he said. "Yup, they're right over there."

Farr approached the couple, displayed his badge, and asked them to sit in his car to be interviewed.

Wes Burt gave him the following information:

The couple had paid $100,000 down and mortgaged their two-hundred-acre farm to buy the foundry a year earlier, but had run into problems that led them to lay off their production crew ten days before the fire. In an effort to hang on to their most important customers, several nationally known fishing boat manufacturers, Burt had met with two executives from a competing aluminum foundry based in Nixa. He'd driven to the Steak and Ale Restaurant in Springfield the day before the fire to meet with them.

Wes Burt met with Roger Moore, president of Springfield Aluminum, and Gerald Carnahan, an executive and the son of the owner. Burt had made his pitch and named his price. He asked the Nixa foundry to make the parts for the boat manufacturer using the sand molds that were already stored at his foundry in Aurora. That way he could keep his customers happy and hopefully they would place more orders through his business. But Moore, a cautious, careful type probably quite unlike his namesake, actor Roger Moore of James Bond fame, called him the next day and said the Nixa foundry was going to decline the offer.

However, the supervisor of another aluminum foundry, this one in Coffeyville, Kansas, accepted the deal after Burt called with his offer. The Burts would use their truck the next day to deliver the sand cast molds that would be used to make the boat parts. In fact, that very night, hours before the fire, their son had gone to the foundry to get the truck so they could start out early in the morning for Kansas. But it wouldn't start because of a dead battery. They decided to wait until morning to fix the truck.

And then the fire department had called.

The firm had a storage facility, a defunct and decrepit former foundry in Verona, five miles west of Aurora. Here they stored hundreds of other sand cast molds on loan from boat companies.

Farr figured that despite the odd things found at the Aurora fire, the thief had to have some connection to the aluminum foundry business to risk breaking in and lugging dozens of molds. And if he knew that, he might know that the Burts stored more molds elsewhere.

Bill Farr asked Wes Burt to ride with him to the old foundry in Verona. When they pulled up to the front door they saw the padlock hasp was sawed in two and the still-locked padlock was lying on the ground. But the door showed no signs of being forced. The building was dark because the power was off.

Burt used his key to get inside. Immediately, Farr saw

footprints left by someone who had been walking in soft earth or mud. The prints matched those left at the Aurora fire. However, nothing was missing. There was no vandalism, no spray paint or anything else weird. The prints led into an office and then back out again to the door with the broken hasp.

Farr asked Burt exactly how a sand cast mold was used. What he learned narrowed the pool of suspects. Each mold was unique to a certain part of a manufacturer's assembly line. While many types of fishing boats are similar, they are not identical. The molds taken in Aurora were imprinted with serial numbers in such a way that they could not be altered. They could be used only to produce a specific part for a specific manufacturer.

A thief would not be able to sell the molds except to a foundry. And then, any informed foundry operator would want to know how he got them. The only value they might present would be to another foundry that made parts for the same manufacturers. And to use them in that manner would require a shady deal.

Farr wondered about the red paint and spilled ink. Why had the thief been so careless? Why had he left near-perfect footprints and his bolt cutters at the crime scene? This didn't sound like a professional.

It was possible, Farr knew, that some inexperienced burglar came upon the sand cast molds and figured they must be valuable, not knowing they were stamped with serial numbers and only loaned out to foundries. But that wouldn't explain how the same burglar knew about the

Burts' storage facility at the old Verona foundry. That was insider information.

A ransom was possible, he thought. But that seemed like such a long shot. How much ransom would be paid on $50,000 or $60,000 worth of manufacturing molds?

Farr knew his suspect must have had a motive to brazenly break into a foundry and set it on fire. But that motive didn't necessarily have to make sense . . .

CHAPTER 23

- - - ——————— - - -

HEAVY LOAD

The new Chrysler minivan was so heavily loaded it hunkered down inches from the pavement like kind of a corporate low rider. Springfield Aluminum owned it, but Gerry Carnahan was the only one who drove it. He usually kept it at home until he came into the office at his regular time of around 9 A.M.

But on this day, September 18, 1993, at only 7 A.M. the white van was parked in Gerry's regular spot one over from company president Roger Moore.

When Moore pulled up at his own normal arrival time of 7 A.M. he felt apprehensive. He wondered what craziness his boss's son had undertaken during the night that would make the company van ride so low. *And what was Gerry doing at work at such an early hour*?

Moore's routine was to arrive an hour before the office opened at 8 A.M. so he could catch up on messages.

Sometimes Carnahan didn't come in at all. But here he was. Two hours early. And as Moore would later recount to police, it had to mean trouble.

In the ten years he had worked for the company, Moore had come to fear Gerry Carnahan, who was a decade his junior. The newspaper headlines about Carnahan being suspected of murdering women all over the Ozarks was just a part of it. Moore knew from working with him that Carnahan's temper could erupt at the slightest provocation.

Gerry Carnahan was a mean, spoiled, overgrown brat who had to be endured because his father owned the company. That was what everybody knew but nobody talked about unless they were sure none of the Carnahan family or their spies were around to hear.

Moore recalled a story that involved Carnahan and his parking place, the spot right beside his own.

It was a tale well known throughout the company.

The story went like this: One day the husband of one of the Carnahan company's secretaries parked a delivery van in Carnahan's spot. And that just wasn't done. Carnahan's name was clearly marked on the space. The husband worked for another firm that regularly made deliveries to Springfield Aluminum. His wife was inside working at her desk.

When Carnahan showed up and saw somebody's car in his space, he blocked the guy's car with his own vehicle. He put his bumper right against the guy's car so it couldn't move except to go forward through the shrubbery. The guy came out, saw what had happened, and started swearing.

Carnahan came out, too, and stood nose to nose with the secretary's husband and then got in his own van and chased the guy around the parking lot. Witnesses said he was trying to run him over. The guy ran for his life. Finally, Carnahan allowed him to leave, but it didn't end there. He wouldn't let it alone. He called the man's boss, and before the poor guy got back to his job he had been fired.

Another time, chaos had erupted because of Carnahan when he'd begun harassing "Bud," a production guy who worked in the foundry, during a return trip from a golf outing in St. Louis. The way the story had been told to Moore, Carnahan, maybe feeling the effects of one too many beers, grabbed Bud's baseball cap and wouldn't give it back. When Carnahan threatened to throw it out the window, Bud, who was sitting in the back, reached into the front seat and took it back. But, as he did, Carnahan kissed him on the cheek and fists flew. They got to pounding on each other so hard that one of them kicked the windshield out right on I-44 West at sixty-five miles per hour. A car had to be sent from Nixa to get them.

Married with five kids, Roger Moore had worked as a certified public accountant for big companies in California. He had a master's degree in accounting from Caltech. He had taught accounting and started up his own software company, which he sold to come and work for Springfield Aluminum. He started as chief financial officer and in just over a year, Garnett Carnahan made him president. But he had never met anyone so dangerously out of control, he would later tell police, as Garnett's son Gerry Carnahan.

Back in 1985, Sheriff Dwight McNiel and Detective Rodney Burk had questioned Moore about the Jackie Johns murder. Jackie had worked briefly for the company in the factory section but quit after only a few months. She had expected to be assigned to a secretarial job in the front office and hadn't liked working on the assembly line. Moore was certain that there had been no romantic involvement between Carnahan and Jackie. Moore told the officers he'd never seen them together.

Now, eight years later, Moore entered the darkened office building and opened the door to his office, not knowing what to expect. He flipped on the lights. Sprawled out on Moore's sofa lay Carnahan, sound asleep. The details of what happened next would eventually be transcribed by a police stenographer while Moore underwent questioning.

Carnahan turned over and opened one eye. Moore would remember the conversation in detail when asked about it the next day.

"Gerry, I can leave and come back," said Moore, who remained standing, wondering what turmoil was about to face him because of his boss's crazy son. "Do you have an early morning visit with a customer? I see that the van's all loaded up."

Carnahan sat up. He looked haggard, as if he'd been out drinking all night.

"No, I don't have to see a customer. I picked up some tooling at Custom Foundries last night."

"How'd you do that?" said Moore, who had been at the meeting at Steak and Ale, and had personally called Wes Burt at Custom Foundry to turn down the offer.

"Well, I stole it," said Carnahan.

"You mean you just broke in and stole it?"

"Well, I tried to hot-wire the truck or van or whatever it was. I broke the window but I couldn't get it started."

Moore began backing up and reached behind him for the knob on his office door.

"Just go back to sleep, Gerry," he said.

In the parking lot, Moore used his cell phone to call Garnett Carnahan. "Please come right over and handle this right now," he said. He waited anxiously. An hour later Garnett Carnahan showed up and talked with his son. Moore left and went home.

By the end of the day, Moore had consulted his own lawyer by telephone, a friend who still lived in California. His advice: Call the cops. Instead, Moore called the attorney for the owner of Custom Foundry. Then he called the cops. Ten minutes after that, Gerry Carnahan called Moore.

"What did you tell him?" he asked.

Moore said, "I told him what you did. All about it."

"Oh shit," Carnahan said and hung up.

That night, Moore loaded a twelve-gauge pump shotgun. His sons loaded their hunting rifles and kept them close at hand. He and his wife stayed up most of the night, watching from upstairs windows. They kept the lights off except for a single lamp.

As Moore told Bill Farr, the fire marshal, "My boys had their rifles loaded. We locked all the doors. I just hoped nobody came through a window because Gerry Carnahan is a very capable person."

On the day after he had taken Moore's statement and had interviewed other witnesses, Farr's immediate problem involved search warrants. He would need a bunch of them.

Based on his extensive interview with Moore, Farr considered Gerry Carnahan a burglar and an arsonist who needed to be arrested. But those stolen sand castings were evidence. They were not in the van and still had to be found. Farr suspected that Carnahan had hidden the castings at one of the many outbuildings and storage sheds owned by the family's company at various locations. Or they might be at his farmhouse in Springfield.

Once a judge signed the search warrants, more than thirty cops—members of the Highway Patrol, investigators from the office of the state fire marshal, and local officers—fanned out in the early morning hours two days after the arson fire in Aurora. The main target was Gerry Carnahan's house, and here special precautions were taken.

Farr, who coordinated the search, told his officers to surround the farmhouse at discreet locations. He went with Springfield cops to the front door where they served Carnahan with the warrant. He was asked to step outside. But no stolen items were found. Carnahan was quiet and offered no trouble. He declined to be interviewed unless his attorney was present.

Searches at the other locations, including rural storage sheds and even a swimming pool, also came up empty.

Nevertheless, on September 20, 1993, three days after the fire, arrest warrants were issued charging Gerry Carnahan with felony counts of arson, burglary, and theft. But he couldn't be found. A few days later, however, he turned up at the Lawrence County courthouse, telling sheriff's deputies he had been unaware that warrants had been issued for his arrest. He was arrested on the spot and held in the county jail.

A few days later he appeared before associate circuit judge Sam Jones.

County prosecutor Robert George asked Jones to hold Carnahan on $90,000 bail because he might flee, given that he also had a separate trial scheduled to begin the following month in Greene County on the charge that he tried to kidnap Heather Starkey.

But Jones set bail at $40,000, of which only 10 percent or $4,000 had to be put up in cash. Minutes later, after one of the lawyers from his legal team showed up, Carnahan laid forty $100 bills on the desk of a clerk in the circuit clerk's office and walked out of the courthouse. A clerk remembered that he said, "Have a nice day."

The lawyer had used Gerry Carnahan's new gold Cadillac (the same car Carnahan had used to drive reporter Ron Davis to lunch in) to drive to Mt. Vernon. Carnahan had asked him to bring the Caddy and a change of clothes. Then, after changing into a sports jacket and slacks, Carnahan slid across the white leather of the driver's seat and drove off with his attorney.

Farr watched him drive away. He told a highway patrolman who was at the courthouse, "You'd think that guy was superman the way people treat him. He's got those big dollar lawyers. The ones that tear you apart on the stand and then pat you on the back afterward."

Farr knew his job wasn't over. There would be a trial in Lawrence County, and he had to get ready for that. There would be laboratory testing of the bolt cutters and other evidence. His report of the fire would eventually reach sixty-five pages.

However, there was something else. And that was murder. Farr knew about Carnahan's reputation as a suspected serial killer and the prime suspect in the Jackie Johns case. He was intrigued and, like any good cop, was open to any information about additional crimes.

Murder came up in connection with the fire investigation when an employee of the foundry in Nixa called and asked for a secret meeting with Farr. The employee made Farr promise never to reveal his name except to investigators he trusted. The man said again and again that Gerry Carnahan would kill him if he ever found out that he was talking to Farr. It was obvious that the employee feared for his life, but Farr had a hard time believing that one man, even someone as apparently unstable as Carnahan, could instill that much fear in anyone. Still, he knew that Roger Moore, the company president, had also been worried enough to arm himself with a shotgun and stay up all night guarding his house after he had told investigators what Carnahan had said.

The foundry worker gave Farr directions to his house, some twenty miles east of Nixa. When Farr arrived, the man waved him inside and pointed to where he should sit. The man described for Farr how aluminum melted at a high temperature, 1,220 degrees Fahrenheit; enough heat to consume just about anything. But the man said he had once seen something in the silvery liquid of the Springfield Aluminum melting vat that had shocked him. It looked like chunks of bone. They had bubbled to the top and then sank out of sight. He never saw them again, but he was sure they were bones. Exactly what types of bones were in the melting pot couldn't be determined. Whatever they were, he said they caused the melt to test badly. The aluminum's chemical content, measured on a special machine, had come up out of whack. They couldn't use that batch.

The man said he believed Gerry Carnahan had kidnapped that woman and the two young girls who went missing from Springfield in 1992, and that when he was finished with them, pitched their corpses into the vat of molten metal.

It was a mighty tall tale, but the man was convinced

of what he thought had happened. However, he had not the slightest bit of physical evidence, which made it hard to believe based on common sense factors, such as, how could one man, even a reputed crazy man like Carnahan, tote three dead (or bound) women to his father's business (where watchmen were on duty twenty-four hours a day) and slide them unnoticed into a vat?

And yet, as Farr drove home along the shadowy narrow road, he let his mind wander. The tale about the chunks of bone swirling in the bubbling pool of aluminum was unnerving. He didn't know what to believe when it came to Gerry Carnahan.

CHAPTER 24

THE CHAMELEON

"If I did all the things they say I did, I'd have no time for fishing."

In late 1993, a disastrous year for Gerald Carnahan, that curious quotation became part of his defense. When the barrage of news stories about him intensified, or when reporters tried to corner him on the street, he'd utter one of his homey platitudes.

"I'm just a businessman trying to make a living," he might say, or "Ease up on this old dog."

Facing trials for the attempted kidnapping of a young girl, for arson, and for assaulting police officers, Carnahan tried to offset the poisonous publicity generated by headline after headline and countless stories on the evening news. He never missed a chance to tell a reporter that he was just a regular guy, a businessman who went to work every day to make an honest living. The quotes showed up in print and on television.

"I'm just an average guy," he might say.

As of late November, just before the Heather Starkey attempted kidnapping trial was set to start, no actual evidence proved Gerald Carnahan had murdered anyone. In fact, he had no convictions for any type of crime. Carnahan pushed back whenever he could. After one of his innumerable court appearances, when he stepped back onto the street, he would sometimes face his media entourage, his face deadpan, and insist that he was completely puzzled why folks from an entire region thought that he was some kind of a murderous stalker who preyed on young women.

Reporters like Ron Davis of the *Springfield News-Leader*, who knew Carnahan well, didn't bother to write in their notebooks or turn on their microphones when they heard such utterances. They had heard it all before. Only neophytes wrote down his every word.

By the time Gerry Carnahan and his lawyer Jack Yocom showed up at the Boone County courthouse in Columbia for the first day of the attempted kidnapping trial, adjectives like "notorious" and "infamous" regularly turned up in print and during television and radio broadcasts.

However, as he had managed to do numerous times, Carnahan pulled his chameleon trick, the one where he turned back into proper businessman and regular guy. Sure, he might've been wild-eyed and drunk as a skunk back in July 1992 when his wife Pat called the cops to their home in Springfield. He had fired a pistol shot into the floor just before officers showed up, at least according to the criminal complaint that followed. He had kicked one officer and tossed a foam cup of his urine at another. (If he was asked why he was walking around his apartment with a cup of urine, the police report made no mention of it.) Police had arrested and charged him with assault.

And Carnahan had treated his wife badly, according to the order of protection she'd filed on November 18, 1992, at the courthouse in Springfield. Her handwritten description, filed in support of an order that a judge signed that day, described a sadistic, out-of-control drug abuser.

Outlining a series of events that began in April 1990, Collins wrote that Carnahan attacked her, vowing, as she struggled to twist free, to give her a sexually transmitted disease. She wrote that in 1991 he had used a television remote like a whip to repeatedly strike her in the face and legs. Then later that year he burned her with a hot iron, an attack that resulted in Collins calling 911.

Her account stated that he ran over her foot with his car and then used an iron rod to vandalize her own vehicle.

"Respondent has threatened to kill petitioner's father," the complaint stated. Collins's plea for protection went on to say that he said he wouldn't kill her ". . . because he couldn't make her suffer enough."

She claimed Carnahan beat her again and again. "There are many other instances of physical abuse by respondent to petitioner too numerous to mention," she wrote.

And during all this time, Collins alleged, her husband was taking prescription medicines without the knowledge of a physician. She listed these as Xanax, Halcion, and Prozac.

Despite these horrendous accusations, two weeks later she asked without explanation to withdraw the protection order. The judge approved her request.

To see Carnahan as newspaper reporter Ron Davis did on the first day of the attempted kidnapping trial in Columbia, smiling and smug in an expensive camel's hair suit, an unknowing outsider might have a hard time believing that Gerry Carnahan could be involved in such ugliness. He was now thirty-five, though after gaining twenty pounds and a paunch, looked about forty, and no more threatening than one of the Rotarians who regularly showed up at a business lunch down the street from the courthouse.

And there was an underside to the court proceedings leading to the trial that fleshed out Carnahan's camouflaged weirdness even further. It was part of an undercurrent of legal wrangling that hadn't made the television news, although Davis reported some of it in the newspaper.

One example was the plan to cruise to the Bahamas. On April 13, 1993, while his client was free on $15,000 bail for the attempted kidnapping, Yocom had filed a motion asking trial judge Frank Conley to allow Carnahan and his wife to go on a weeklong cruise through the

Caribbean, leaving Fort Lauderdale on April 20, despite the fact that Carnahan's bail restrictions, which included not drinking alcohol and not committing new crimes, also prohibited travel out of state. Still, Yocom wrote that his client stood to lose the $1,500 he had paid for the trip unless the judge allowed the cruise.

Judge Conley denied the motion and further ordered Carnahan to surrender his passport.

In a more chilling example, that August Carnahan had tried to contact Cynthia Rushevsky, the assistant prosecutor in the Starkey kidnapping case. It sent alarm signals throughout the courthouse. Rushevsky had been shocked when one of her receptionists handed her the phone and said, "It's that guy Gerry Carnahan." She had refused to accept it and instead wrote a letter to Carnahan's attorney Jack Yocom asking him to order his client to stop trying to call her. Prosecutors must refrain from any contact with a defendant unless his attorney is present. Besides, Rushevsky was well aware of the dark side of Gerry Carnahan. She didn't want any phone calls from him.

The pretrial tussles focused on whether Carnahan was such a threat he should have his bail revoked. Rushevsky wanted him behind bars until the end of the trial. She called him a "dangerous individual to the citizens of southwest Missouri . . . [who] needs to be incarcerated."

To back up her argument, she told Judge Conley that while out on bail Carnahan had been charged with two misdemeanors for assaulting police officers, and three felonies: the arson, burglary, and theft charges in connection to the break-in at the foundry in Aurora. Bail had been set at $40,000 in that case, which Carnahan had easily managed to cover with a pocketful of hundred-dollar bills.

Then, a couple of months after the attempt to call Rushevsky in August, there was a fracas involving Carnahan and an unrelated fire in his own neighborhood. Carnahan and his wife had moved from the farmhouse on South National Road to South Devon in another part of Springfield. On October 22, 1993, while Rushevsky was waiting for Conley to rule on her motion, a house just down the steeply inclined street from the Carnahan's home caught fire, and onlookers gathered to watch firemen battle the blaze.

On that day, Cory White, who lived nearby, saw the smoke. She drove her Geo Tracker to South Devon and parked in front of Carnahan's house to watch. She left her car door unlocked.

Her boyfriend Sean McQueary, who had ridden with her, was standing nearby when Carnahan came down from his porch, can of beer in hand, and, without a word, got behind the wheel of White's car.

"Hey, what are you doing?" McQueary had shouted. Carnahan ignored him and released the car's emergency brake. He then jumped out and watched the vehicle roll past the firemen and careen down a steep hill. White, who had walked closer to the burning house, watched in horror as her driverless car smacked into a tree and then slammed into a brick retaining wall. It was a total wreck.

When confronted by an angry McQueary, Carnahan said nonchalantly, "I just don't care."

He was charged that day with felony tampering with a motor vehicle but again was released from police custody, putting up $500 cash bond to cover bail set at $5,000. Again, he paid in hundred-dollar bills.

When she heard about the incident with the car, Rushevsky updated her motion to Judge Conley to include the felony tampering charge, and asked that he rule quickly. He did, but not in her favor. Carnahan remained free on bond. Rushevsky warned her assistants to be extremely vigilant around the courthouse and especially when they walked to their vehicles in the adjacent parking lot. She feared that Carnahan was out of control.

The victim of the attempted kidnapping, eighteen-year-old Heather Starkey, told prosecutors that she didn't want to testify because she feared Gerry Carnahan. She had heard the broadcast reports and read the newspaper accounts. She knew he was the top suspect in the murder of Jackie Johns. Starkey had balked during depositions taken by the defense, answering some questions only reluctantly.

"I don't see how that's relevant," she told Yocom when he asked during a deposition what she and her boyfriend had been fighting about when she insisted on being let out of his car.

On Wednesday, December 1, 1993, the day the kidnapping trial began, reporter Ron Davis positioned himself in the front row of spectators, as close to Gerry

Carnahan as he could get. He carefully noted where Carnahan's wife, Pat Collins, sat. Stepdaughter Sara, who'd been found not guilty of perjury five years earlier, regarding her statement to police that Carnahan was home with her the night Jackie disappeared, did not attend his trial. He spotted Jackie's widowed father Les Johns near the front. He noted that Pam Workman sat nearby. She told friends she was convinced that Carnahan had murdered her sister Kelle who had disappeared five years earlier from a cemetery in Christian County while mowing grass.

The opening statements were brief. Prosecutor Cynthia Rushevsky said eyewitnesses, including the victim herself, would tell a tale of terror. Defense attorney Jack Yocom, his voice carrying throughout the courtroom, said his client had only attempted to help a young woman he saw walking alone early in the morning along a dark highway in the sleet and cold.

The highlight of the first day was more than an hour of testimony from Heather Starkey.

She wore a blue sailor suit and began crying just after she put her hand on a Bible and swore to tell the truth. Rushevsky handled the direct examination.

Davis took careful notes that he would use in his story. He quoted Heather Starkey:

"I went out with my boyfriend to a going away party for a couple of his friends . . . We were there about four hours, maybe longer. I had approximately a cup-and-a-half of beer all night. We got into an argument but I don't remember what we argued about."

Heather got to the part about slapping her boyfriend and being let out of his car. Davis kept writing.

"A white car passed and pulled into the first apartment complex driveway. The defendant got out of the passenger side, but I assumed they were just dropping him off. I'd never seen him before."

When she got to the part where Carnahan came at her, she began to sob louder.

"He grabbed my right arm. I was screaming. 'Stop. Please stop! No! Get away!' He made no effort to back away.

"Then he had both hands on my upper arms. We were moving toward a field and some woods. We fell. He fell on his left-hand side. I fell with my knees down. I got up quicker than he did. I just got up and ran. I looked back and he was just getting up. I ran even faster."

Davis noted that the courtroom, which he described as "cavernous," was hushed while Heather Starkey described the attack. That changed in a moment when Yocom got his turn at the witness.

He zeroed in on the difference between what she told the police and what she had just testified to in court. Yocom, his voice booming against the twenty-five-foot-high ceiling, said, "Why did you tell the police he was trying to drag you to his car? You just said it was toward the woods."

Heather answered that she didn't know why her accounts were contradictory. But she said she was sure he had been trying to drag her to the woods.

She'd also later found scratches on her back but didn't

initially tell the police about them because, as she told Yocom, "I didn't think it was a big deal."

"Her story is kind of like old wine, it gets better with age," Yocom told the jury. Rushevsky objected.

Yocom said, "Withdrawn," before Conley could rule on the objection.

Heather told the jurors she couldn't remember certain details about the attack. And each time she did, Yocom shouted, "You don't remember? Is your memory that bad?"

Davis wrote furiously. He watched Heather clench her jaw under the questioning. He wrote, "She held her ground."

The apparent contradiction in her testimony—was it toward the woods or toward the car—would become a key issue. If Carnahan was trying to force her into the woods, would he have done so while his friend, the driver of the rented Chrysler, could see him?

Liz Zaagsma, the woman who told police she saw Carnahan struggling with Heather Starkey and who had managed to write down the license plate of the Chrysler, also withstood Yocom's questioning. While her account contained inconsistencies as well, she patiently pointed out that there were more facts that she got right than could be wrong.

On the second day of the trial, Davis got there early to make sure he got a front-row seat.

The expectation was that Carnahan himself would take the stand. Court watchers predicted that he would. But Yocom decided against that.

If Carnahan took the stand, his fragile claim that he had merely told his friend to stop and let him out so he could help Heather Starkey would be subject to a savage cross-examination. Yocom knew Rushevsky was prepared to rip this claim to shreds.

Carnahan had also told police he simply slipped on the sleet-covered ground and had grabbed the girl to keep himself from falling. That didn't explain the scratches on her back or the terror she had endured. Why would he pull her toward the woods if he was going to help her?

The jury was out for just over three hours. Davis, who was waiting in a restaurant across the street from the courthouse, got a call from a court bailiff. The jury had sent the judge a note. They had a verdict.

The players took their positions in the courtroom. Yocom sat beside Carnahan at the defense table. Rushevsky and her assistant were seated at a table ten feet away. Conley, in his black robe, strode in from a door behind the bench. The bailiff called out, "All rise!"

The onlookers and court personnel remained standing, as did the judge, while the twelve jurors and two alternates filed in and stood in front of their assigned seats in the jury box.

Conley said, "Please be seated."

Once again, Davis got the best seat. He knew he would hear the judge read the verdict. But what he wanted to see was the reaction of certain onlookers, namely Carnahan's wife Pat, Jackie's father Les Johns, and Kelle Workman's sister Pam. He turned in his seat to watch them.

Conley read the verdict. It was guilty, with a jury recommendation of two years in state prison. Carnahan had faced seven years.

Davis's front-page story the next morning would lead the paper. He wrote, "And as the judge read the jury's decision, several things happened. Pat Collins's right hand formed a fist then relaxed, as she looked impassively at her emotionless husband.

"Pam Workman's eyes reddened. For the thousandth time this day she thought of her dead sister Kelle, and wondered whether Carnahan killed her. And Les Johns snapped to in his seat and smiled, because here was the news he had craved since 1985, when the battered body of his daughter Jackie was pulled from Lake Springfield."

Davis's story, written on deadline and sent by laptop to the *News-Leader* 150 miles away, captured what the citizens of Springfield and especially the residents of Nixa would undoubtedly feel when they heard the news. And what Les Johns felt and had savored when he heard the word "guilty."

"No longer was Gerald Carnahan a larger-than-life local legend, notorious for his ability to frustrate cops who suspect him of murder. Now, he was simply a convicted felon," Davis wrote.

Judge Conley set a sentencing date for January 1994.

But just nine days after his conviction, Gerry Carnahan was interviewed by Davis and the story again led the front page.

"I love the Springfield area. But I don't think I'll ever beat the negative feeling some people have for me," he said. "I'm just an average guy."

Few were convinced. Carnahan had just been convicted of trying to drag a teenage girl into the woods. That conviction made the leap to believing he'd killed Jackie Johns, and probably others, that much easier.

Davis, who had been sternly ordered by his editor to get to know Carnahan better than any other reporter, may have said it best in this story.

"You should see the looks he gets," the story began. Davis went on to describe how people stared at Gerry Carnahan wherever he went in public, recognizing him from television or newspaper photos.

"But for the aggressive ones," his story continued, "looking isn't enough. They get in front of Carnahan and say to his face what many more whisper behind his back.

"Murderer. You're a murderer."

CHAPTER 25

TIME OUT

Two or three times a night, Gerry Carnahan would call reporter Ron Davis of the *Springfield News-Leader*, who probably knew him better than anyone outside his family. The calls came from the Greene County jail. After the Starkey trial, Carnahan had pleaded guilty to the arson in Aurora and his bail was revoked.

Years later, even after Davis moved on to become a senior producer at a television station in Springfield, he still often talked about Carnahan. Davis said he'd accepted the calls. His wife, an editor at the paper, was tolerant of the nightly interruptions. Lou Ziegler, her husband's editor, had insisted Davis get to know Carnahan better than any other reporter. That wouldn't stop just because Carnahan's bail had finally been revoked and he was awaiting sentencing on the felony tampering charge for sending the Geo Tracker down a hill.

And there was always the chance, Davis thought, that Carnahan might drop an inadvertent bomb, a clue that might lead to solving the Debbie Sue Lewis murder, or the case of the three missing women, Springfield's most baffling crime. Or maybe what happened to Kelle Workman.

But the calls were bizarre.

One night Carnahan called and asked Davis to come around to the side of the jail and toss a bag of cigarettes over the wall.

"You know I can't do that, Gerry," Davis said.

Another night the talk was all about driving.

"Where would you go?" Davis asked.

"I don't know. I guess I'd just drive," Carnahan said. "I guess that would be the beauty of it. Not knowing where you're going."

He sent letters. Many were signed, "The Guv," a take on the fact that the Missouri governor at the time was Mel Carnahan, a Democrat who had been elected the year before, despite there being no relation between them.

Gerry Carnahan's lawyer Jack Yocom was interviewed by newspaper and television reporters and asked what he thought of his client, who had finally been convicted of not one but four felonies.

"He will have to accept it and change for the better," said Yocom, always the optimist.

Davis detected growing frustration in some of the calls.

Carnahan would shout, "Shut the fuck up," to his

cellmates, and then apologize to Davis for cursing. Finally, after a few weeks, the calls trickled to one or two every other day and then stopped altogether.

Carnahan was sentenced to a year in prison on the felony tampering with an automobile charge. All in all, his sentences for attempted kidnapping, arson, and destroying the car added up to four convictions and seven years. The judges ran them concurrent, however, which meant his sentence was four years overall. With time off for good behavior, he would be released in just over two years.

In January of 1994, jailers told Carnahan to be ready. He'd be making the move to prison. When his time came, it was 5 A.M. The lights came on.

"Carnahan, roll up," a guard shouted.

A trusty, an inmate serving a short sentence in the county jail, brought him a breakfast tray. It consisted of a cup of grapefruit, scrambled eggs, a carton of milk, and toast. He ate it all.

Minutes later, they came for him. A security chain was attached to his waist and his hands were cuffed to metal links in such a way that if he leaned way forward he could just manage to scratch his nose.

And then Gerry Carnahan was loaded into a van with two other prisoners. The ride to the Fulton Reception and Diagnostic Center took nearly two and a half hours.

———

A little over two years later, on April 7, 1996, a guard pushed a piece of paper across a Formica counter at the

Western Missouri Correctional Center near Kansas City. Gerald Carnahan dutifully waited behind a yellow line painted on the floor five feet away. He made sure his toes did not actually touch the line. It was a rule he had strictly obeyed during his time behind bars.

"All right. You, c'mon," the guard said. Carnahan stepped forward. He placed a plastic bag containing his possessions on the counter to be searched.

"Sign on the dotted line," he was told.

In return for his signature, he was given another plastic bag marked "Missouri State Penitentiary." In it was a new sports jacket, dress shirt, slacks, socks, and underwear. The price tags were still attached. His family had had the clothing delivered to the relatively modern lockup in preparation for this day when he was scheduled to be released.

Carnahan quickly dressed while the guard went through the bag of possessions he would be allowed to take with him. It wasn't much of a collection, mostly legal papers and letters. While he was locked up, Pat Collins had divorced him, filing a petition citing him for "mental cruelty" at a courthouse in Nevada, a city in Vernon County. The divorce went into effect on June 6, 1995, nearly ten years after Jackie Johns's murder.

Despite his bad-boy reputation, Carnahan had spent his stint without trouble. He hadn't fought with other inmates or with guards. He managed to keep all his good time.

But he wasn't going to walk out of the prison a free man. Instead, he was released to detainers, or criminal charges put on hold by Greene County in connection with his convictions on misdemeanors for assaulting a police officer and brandishing a pistol while drunk.

Two deputies were waiting for him when he walked out of the prison's main gate. He stopped and took a deep breath. Behind him, the rows and rows of razor wire at the prison were bathed in the morning sunlight. But Carnahan didn't look back. He nodded to the Greene County deputies, who were there to take him to the county jail in Springfield to serve the remaining fifteen months of his sentence. He held out his wrists to be handcuffed. They cuffed them in front, a kindness. It would have been very painful to sit in the back of a police cruiser with his hands behind him on the long ride back to Springfield.

"Watch your head," a deputy said as Carnahan got in the backseat.

During the two-and-a-half-hour drive, they ignored him and talked only between themselves.

Instead of the media attention he was used to, Carnahan's arrival went unnoticed except for a story buried on an inside page in the *Springfield News-Leader* the next morning, April 8, 1996, under the headline "Criminal returns to city for more jail time."

Not "Carnahan returns," or "Suspected serial killer," or any of the lurid headlines that once elevated Gerry Carnahan to the status of the town's most dangerous guy.

The story was by Ron Davis, Carnahan's favorite chronicler. But the old mystique around Carnahan was gone. This story was straight nuts and bolts without Davis's usual flair and eye for detail.

Former sheriff Dwight McNiel read it. So did Tom Martin, who had retired from the Highway Patrol. McNiel had stopped thinking of himself as a "nail" being driven into obscurity by an unseen hammer. He was doing well. Great, in fact.

He now owned his own private detective agency, Midwest Intelligence. Gone were McNiel & Associates and the one-room apartment with no phone. His agency was the real thing with an office and investigators who worked for him. He had the satisfaction of seeing his children become successful in their own careers.

He'd remarried to a woman named Marcella, a paralegal whose law firm once hired him to investigate a suspected insurance fraud scam. A guy had received a seven-figure settlement for a back injury that supposedly disabled him, yet McNiel videotaped him for several days sitting in a bass boat on a Missouri lake, pulling in fish during a fishing tournament.

McNiel had a beautiful home in Ozark and a sixty-five-foot houseboat that he docked on Table Rock Lake and called "The Private Aye." It was air-conditioned with a meeting room for clients and a fully equipped kitchen.

But McNiel hadn't forgotten about Carnahan. Neither had Martin. Both kept in touch with police friends still on the job, hoping to hear that investigators had developed a new lead in the Jackie Johns murder. Or in the Debbie Sue Lewis case. Or in any unsolved murder of women in the Nixa/Springfield area that might have been the work of Carnahan. But none had.

McNiel heard that Pat Collins divorced Gerry Carnahan while he was in prison, filing the paperwork in another county to avoid publicity. The listed reason, he found when he checked it out, was "mental cruelty."

In September 1997, when Carnahan finished his county jail time and was finally freed, McNiel used his private investigation connections to track him. He learned that Carnahan had left the country for Taiwan on what was supposed to be an extended buying trip for the family aluminum business, though McNiel heard he'd been sent abroad to keep out of trouble. Trying to keep tabs on him there was nearly impossible.

By 1997, Nixa was the epicenter of growth in southwestern Missouri. The town had tripled in size since Jackie Johns was murdered, spurred by the wild popularity of the showbiz entertainment center in Branson just to the south. The 7-11, once the social center for Jackie and her friends, had become just another roadside convenience store. Malls and fast-food restaurants sprouted up all around. Young people went to hang out there instead of the 7-11.

The Nixa Sucker Day festival was still held every May, but the number of people who attended the one-day event at its peak, when Jackie Johns was chosen queen, began to drop off. The organizers were lucky to get seven or eight thousand people to show up to buy fried sucker sandwiches and drink beer and pump money into the town's economy. It used to bring in fifteen thousand people.

Jackie's friends went on with their lives, although that night in June 1985 when she disappeared was not forgotten. The Sale Barn Café still drew hordes of customers. Jackie was still talked about, although new customers had to be told who she was.

Jackie's best friend Lisa Fitzpatrick married and became Lisa Shaw. She had three children. Even years after Jackie's murder, when she was an adult with children of her own, Lisa's father still called and warned her to be careful whenever she went out at night.

Jackie's other best friend, Dayna Spencer, first worked for the Nixa Police Department, then for several years as a Christian County deputy sheriff. Whenever she went on patrol late at night, she regularly looked for Carnahan's car, but had never spotted it.

"I had a fantasy that I would have some legal reason to pull him over and then he would pull a weapon and I'd have cause to shoot him," she once told Lisa. "But that was silly. Just daydreams."

The two friends possessed dozens of snapshots of Jackie and themselves taken with boys they had known. Sometimes, but not often, they got together to reminisce. Lisa remembered the Sin Wagon, her mother's station wagon, and the times boys chased them in their cars. Nixa wasn't the same without Jackie. But then again, Nixa had changed on its own.

Dayna eventually left police work and signed on with McNiel's private investigation company.

Shirley Johns had died in 1988 of lung cancer. But Les Johns always said she grieved herself to death over the violent end of her youngest child's life. He doggedly kept his daughter in the headlines, hoping that the publicity would somehow lead to Carnahan's arrest for her murder. Les was featured in a front-page story on Father's Day of 1990, which he spent at the cemetery beside Jackie's headstone.

In 1992, another story ran on the *News-Leader*'s front page about Les, in which he lamented that Carnahan would never be arrested for the murder. The story ran under the headline "I'll go to my grave with this."

Interest in Jackie Johns's murder had naturally waned over time, even though it was once the most investigated case ever in Christian County. Nor had police made any arrests for the murders of Debbie Sue Lewis or Kelle Workman, or in connection with the case of the three missing women. Carnahan's name had quickly surfaced in connection with the missing women case, as it had in the murders, but these investigations had all turned cold.

By the time he was released from the county jail in the fall of 1997, Gerry Carnahan was on his way to being forgotten.

CHAPTER 26

COLD CASE

Two years later, in 1999, Springfield Police detective Bill Thomas took a shot at reviving the Jackie Johns murder investigation. He sent a vaginal swab taken during autopsy to the Highway Patrol Crime Lab in Jefferson City. But, at the time, no semen was detected and no DNA testing was done.

The case went back onto the shelf until 2002, when Springfield Police sergeant Brian DiSylvester was assigned to the cold case. He began by inventorying more than four hundred pieces of evidence gathered seventeen years earlier. He replaced torn envelopes and cracked, dried tape. He applied modern bar codes to some of the items to help identify them. Then he started reading.

DiSylvester read the reports off and on for over a year while also working robbery and homicide assignments. The story of the investigation of Jackie's murder was contained in seven large spiral folders. He found time to read several pages each day.

As he turned pages of the reports, DiSylvester tracked the mental descent of Gerald Carnahan. In the many interview transcripts, the murder suspect's darkest side emerged.

In one report, a woman told police about running into Carnahan when both were briefly confined at a Missouri state mental center. She said that sometime in 1991 he had talked then about killing Jackie.

"They're too incompetent to catch me," Carnahan had bragged, she said, according to the typed police account.

The woman had said he told her that he sprayed Jackie with some kind of gas that knocked her out. Then he raped her and beat her to death with her own bumper jack. She said Carnahan claimed he was walking along the road after his truck broke down and Jackie had offered him a lift.

Like everyone who talks to the police, the woman was subject to charges of lying to an officer if it was found that what she talked about in the official report wasn't the truth. Although she wasn't charged, what she said about Carnahan never led to his arrest, either. The account, like other allegations of misconduct and criminality against Carnahan, was never proven.

DiSylvester was struck by some of the other accounts.

There was one dated October 31, 1985, taken during the rush of interviews when Dwight McNiel, the sheriff, and Detective Rod Burk of the Springfield Police questioned more than 150 of Jackie's friends, acquaintances, family members, and coworkers.

When he read this interview, DiSylvester realized that Carnahan simply did what he pleased when it involved a woman.

A twenty-five-year-old woman who had lived with Carnahan a year or two before he married Pat Collins had signed her statement, swearing under penalty of perjury that it was the truth.

The report stated that Burk asked her if Carnahan had any unusual sexual practices. She answered that during the year they lived together in Springfield, Carnahan insisted on sex nearly every day. If she refused, he would masturbate in front of her and then wipe his semen "all over my body," she said.

Even more disturbing, the report went on, the woman told Detective Burk that Carnahan later broke into the trailer she had moved into with another man, and that, one night while they were asleep in bed, she awoke with a start to find Carnahan standing over them. He then removed his clothing and, pinning her arms, raped her as her boyfriend watched in fear.

She had not contacted police because she feared retaliation from Carnahan, the interview stated.

DiSylvester quickly picked up on one eerie detail contained in the report. Burk had asked the woman whether Carnahan ever undressed her in such a way that, during sex, one of the legs of her jeans was rolled up with her panties still in it. She had told Burk that indeed had happened. DiSylvester knew from the case file that was how

Jackie's jeans had been found, with her panties rolled up in one leg.

The case file showed that several women, including at least two former girlfriends, said it was common to see Carnahan with marijuana, although not in great quantity. They also told police he used cocaine and abused antidepressants.

By the time DiSylvester had finished reading the whole file, every instinct told him that Gerry Carnahan was a grave danger to women. He believed it likely that Carnahan had killed and raped Jackie Johns, as investigators had thought all along. He just couldn't prove it. Nothing in the huge file linked Carnahan to any crime that could be proved in a court of law.

Still, years had passed since the last attempt to obtain a DNA profile from the vaginal swab. Genetic profiling techniques had improved. And DiSylvester had obtained a cold case funding grant that was more than enough to pay for advanced testing. As an experienced investigator, he knew that humidity and temperature might already have destroyed any chance of obtaining a DNA profile. But he had to try.

In August of 2003, he sent several pieces of evidence, including the vaginal swab, to ReliaGene Technologies, Inc., in New Orleans. Law enforcement circles considered the firm to have the most advanced testing capability of any lab in the United States and possibly the world. Progress in genetic testing methods and equipment was coming at a rate that made earlier procedures obsolete, sometimes after only months. The biggest advances were in the area of testing minute quantities of genetic material, like those detectable only under a lab microscope.

Then DiSylvester waited. He did not reveal to anyone outside a close circle of investigators that he had sent the evidence for testing. There was no sense telling Les Johns and Jackie's sisters. They had been disappointed many times before.

DiSylvester didn't have to wait long. On September 10, 2003, he got a report from ReliaGene. The lab technician, Gina Pineda, who also supervised DNA testing, stated in her report that "a minimal number of sperm cells" were found. But unfortunately, the sample was too small and too degraded to generate a DNA profile.

Overall, the report was disappointing but tantalizing. DiSylvester realized that ReliaGene had at least confirmed that seminal material, however minute, existed in the sample. Maybe in a few years, he thought, a newer technique might be found that would work on such a small sample.

He tried other paths in the meantime. Hairs had been found in the Camaro that did not come from Jackie. He sent these off to be reexamined. The Highway Patrol Law in Jefferson City had improved their capacity to examine such evidence. These hairs were compared to hair samples taken from Gerry Carnahan when he had been arrested in 1985 on the tampering with evidence charge.

Three months later those results also came back. The hairs were not Carnahan's.

DiSylvester returned the boxes of reports and evidence to locked storage. The Jackie Johns investigation officially returned to the frustrating, unfortunate "cold case" status.

CHAPTER 27

BOXED IN

Those who get away with murder must constantly worry that someday, a bored or curious cop will yank open a cardboard box that had been collecting dust for years and discover a piece of overlooked or misunderstood evidence.

And that one little piece will be enough to bring that knock on the door. That hard pounding followed by, "Police! Open up."

Because even after decades pass and it requires a moment or two for some who lived through the event to recall the victim's name; even when time dulls public outrage and evidence gets stored away; even when cops retire or find other jobs—murder is never forgotten.

In October 2006, lined up along a wall of Sergeant Dan Nash's office at Troop D Headquarters of the Missouri State Highway Patrol in Springfield were eight archival boxes, big as banana crates, packed with thick files and sealed envelopes. And all from the Jackie Johns murder investigation that had been turned over to him by the Springfield Police Department.

The thirty-eight-year-old Nash was assigned to the Johns case because of the experience he'd gained from handling more than one hundred homicide investigations in a varied career that included catching cattle rustlers throughout southwestern Missouri. He was also juggling the investigations of a dozen more current murders when he was assigned to the Johns cold case.

On many of the investigative reports, Nash noticed the signature of former Troop D supervising investigator Sergeant Tom Martin, who had retired as a lieutenant seven years earlier. Seeing his friend's name gave Nash confidence that whatever was in the boxes had been recorded accurately and collected properly.

Nash had an aptitude for seemingly hopeless cold case projects like the Jackie Johns case, especially given such a large volume of records gathered over the previous twenty years. It would take a flair for organization to figure how best to proceed, and that suited him.

Having lived in southern Missouri most of his life, Nash was already somewhat familiar with the Jackie Johns case. His family had moved to Missouri from California after his father, a San Francisco police officer, was shot and wounded on duty. Dan Nash, a tall, blond athletic kid who loved the outdoors, was a good fit for the wilds of Missouri. He decided to stay in the Midwest and went to work for the Missouri State Highway Patrol.

When he wasn't on duty working homicides, Nash was a mountain climber. And not just in the Ozarks or the Poconos. He'd climbed in the Himalayas. When he wasn't solving crimes, he laced on climbing boots, strapped metal-toothed crampons to the soles, and traipsed up glaciers and snowfields into the thin air around the altitude where passenger jets cruise.

Nash honed his organizational skills in the Karakoram Range of the Himalayas, particularly on a peak well known in climbing circles but obscure among the general public: Gasherbrum II, the thirteenth highest mountain in the world at 26,362 feet. When Nash stood on its summit, he looked down on Pakistan and China.

Getting up there from base camp took nearly two months of intense organization. Nash and his climbing partners carefully planned their route and methodically climbed to higher and higher altitudes to acclimate to the oxygen-thin air and gain greater lung capacity and stamina, but then knew to descend, in order to recuperate and let additional oxygen-carrying red blood cells form. Then back up again, only higher. They left supplies in tents pitched at various high camps. They charted the weather and watched for dangerous, avalanche-prone areas. Finally, in the early morning darkness, wearing headlamps to guide them, they had made a successful dash to the top, followed by a safe descent.

Besides his full-time Highway Patrol job, Nash also ran two outdoor companies, Satori Adventures and Expeditions, LLC, and Hiking The Ozarks, LLC. In his time off from the Highway Patrol, he guided expeditions to other mountains, including Mt. Kilimanjaro in Tanzania, or on day hikes deep within the national forests of Missouri.

And Nash's skills as a climber informed his investigative work, too. His motto for both his job as a homicide investigator and a climber was "Plan and prepare." The first thing he did was take his own inventory of the evidence.

But before Dan Nash had even opened the first of the Jackie Johns case boxes, he knew the evidence pointed to Gerald Carnahan. That Carnahan was the killer had been talked about for years among members of the Highway Patrol who were frustrated by their inability to gain enough evidence to make an arrest. And Carnahan's name would also come up when investigators talked about other murder victims, like Debbie Sue Lewis, Kelle Workman, and the unsolved disappearance of the three women from Springfield in 1992.

But this was a summit-like problem. Nash realized he couldn't just go out and slap handcuffs on Carnahan any more than he could jog up a Himalayan mountain in tennis shoes. He must first convince a judge there was probable cause that Carnahan had raped and murdered Jackie and should be arrested. Then he could get a warrant. And then the handcuffs could follow.

It took days to sort through the evidence and reports. There were more than 175 transcribed interviews, some of them twenty pages long. Nash arranged the paperwork on long tables in the Troop D Headquarters evidence room. Fellow investigators stopped in to encourage him.

He finally narrowed the mass of reports and potential evidence to what he would focus his investigation on: thirty-one items that he examined, repackaged, and sent to the Highway Patrol Crime Lab in Jefferson City, the state capital. He included empty soda cans; butts from Marlboro cigarettes; Jackie's bloody bra and other items of her clothing; the partial fingerprint from the bulb for the dome light in her Camaro; a dozen bloodstained pieces of fabric from the car's interior; hairs; a man's underwear briefs; and, in a special envelope that held a plastic container, the vaginal swab collected during the autopsy.

The swab was critical. The Highway Patrol Crime Lab had examined it microscopically in 1999, but couldn't find semen and did not attempt a DNA profile. In 2003, ReliaGene, the New Orleans based forensic testing laboratory, found minute traces of semen but said the sample was too small and degraded to come up with a DNA profile. The accompanying documentation showed that the packaged swab had been refrigerated for a time, but then had been stored in an area in the Springfield Police Department evidence room that was not always air conditioned.

While improved techniques had allowed DNA profiles to be developed from such ancient human tissue as Egyptian mummies buried for millennia in a desert, a vaginal swab could decompose in just a few years. Especially in high humidity heat.

But by 2007, the Missouri State Highway Patrol Crime Lab had acquired the very latest equipment. In just the last few years before Nash got the case, DNA testing had been refined to the point that almost a single sperm cell could be replicated until there was enough material to test. On January 31, 2007, Nash sent the package containing the thirty-one items to be tested, including the vaginal swab, to the state crime lab by special courier.

Then it became a waiting game. He had plenty of other cases to keep him busy.

Six weeks later, the supervisor of the state crime lab called Nash. He told him that thirty of the thirty-one pieces of evidence he submitted had not produced anything in the way of evidence that could point to a killer. But incredibly, the remaining piece of evidence, the vaginal swab, had resulted in a sixteen-point DNA profile, nearly the best possible. When the call ended, Nash stood at the window in his office and looked out across the grounds of the Troop D campus. He had the irrefutable scientific imprint of the man who raped and killed Jackie Johns. It was better than a fingerprint. It was better than a smoking gun.

Now, all he needed was a DNA sample from his only real suspect, Gerald Carnahan, to compare to the profile from the swab. It was a good day. A very good day. But he felt better days were coming.

On March 15, 2007, after the state lab had returned the evidence and sent its DNA profile report, Nash drove to Nixa and obtained a voluntary sample of DNA from Cody Wright, Jackie's boyfriend at the time she was murdered. Wright willingly allowed Nash to use cotton swabs to obtain buccal cells from the inside of his mouth. These cells are ideal for DNA testing. Wright's sample was quickly profiled and he was eliminated as a source of the semen found in the vaginal swab.

Gerry Carnahan was next. Nash wanted to apply for a probable cause warrant ordering Carnahan to submit to buccal cell testing. But Nash found out later that day that his suspect was on a business trip to Taiwan, a country with no extradition treaty with the United States. Nash couldn't get the warrant until his man was back on U.S. soil.

Working connections within the U.S. Customs and Border Protection agency, Nash waited for a phone call. It finally came several months later in August.

A customs agent at LaGuardia Airport in New York City called Sergeant Nash at Troop D Headquarters.

"I'm looking at your guy. He's standing in line," the agent said.

Customs then tracked Carnahan to a flight that landed in Springfield, where two Missouri State Highway Patrol undercover detectives waited. But they didn't arrest him. There was still no evidence that he killed Jackie Johns. They simply tailed the company van that had been sent to pick him up.

Nash called a county judge who agreed to immediately sign a search warrant that would compel Carnahan to open his mouth and let the buccal cell samples be taken.

Accompanied by two uniformed Highway Patrol troopers, Nash drove to the parking lot of Springfield

Aluminum in Nixa. Gerry Carnahan was in his office. He looked startled but shook hands with the officers.

"I don't remember you guys," he said.

But when shown the warrant, Carnahan, the badass, thought by many to be a serial killer who had gotten away and would never be caught, sniffled.

"Is this over that Jackie Johns thing?" he said, his voice breaking.

Nash was amazed. Here was a forty-nine-year-old man with tears running down his cheek. And that infamous Gerry Carnahan smirk, the little smile that had shown up in dozens of front-page photographs, was gone. In its place, erased perhaps by years of worry that he would someday have to pay for his crime, was a down-turned mouth set in a heavily jowled face. The officers quickly took the buccal swab. Nash turned to leave the office.

"When do you think the test will be done?" Carnahan said.

"Don't really know. It'll be a while. We're backed up for at least a year," Nash said.

But Nash knew better. The test would be done overnight by one of the best DNA guys in the Highway Patrol.

With the buccal swab sealed in a special envelope, a highway patrolman drove Nash directly to the Springfield Airport. The Troop D aircraft, a Cessna 150, was already on the tarmac, engine running. He got in, strapped on his seat belt, and tucked the envelope into a side pocket in the door for safekeeping. The whole thing had been like climbing in the Himalayas. It took planning, lots of patience, and then, when the summit was close, a quick dash to the top.

CHAPTER 28

FIFTEEN ZEROS

The flight to the crime lab in Jefferson City took about forty-five minutes. Jason Wyckoff, the supervisor of the DNA testing section who would conduct the test, was waiting for the envelope.

It was 4:45 P.M. In fifteen minutes the clerk who kept the evidence check-in log would be going home. General practice at the lab required that only the clerk could log evidence. Budget concerns meant no overtime except for lab analysts.

Minutes earlier, Nash had called. He was on his way from the airport.

"Don't worry, I'll make it," he had said.

Wyckoff knew that if Nash arrived in time, it meant that he'd be spending hours in the lab and would go home late. No problem, he had told Nash. He had taken a call earlier that day from the Highway Patrol in Springfield and knew that what Nash would be bringing him was crucial evidence from a cold case murder that was a priority matter. Nash told him he had a letter-sized, sealed manila envelope holding two small envelopes containing several cotton swabs. Each one was impregnated with the saliva of Gerald Carnahan. Wyckoff would take custody of the evidence after the clerk logged it into the lab system. This was routine.

In the precise, closed world of DNA criminalists, as they prefer to be called rather than technicians or specialists, buccal swabs were highly requested over tissue samples from other parts of a body. Buccal cells from the skin on the inside of the mouth are rich in DNA. They are easily collected and easy to work with.

On Wyckoff's desk lay a single sheet showing a DNA profile of the vaginal swab taken from Jackie during her autopsy on the day her body was retrieved from Lake Springfield. Weeks earlier, Wyckoff had used that twenty-two-year-old degraded sample from the swab to develop a DNA profile from very minute amounts of semen found on the swab. Even though the trace of semen was microscopic and degraded, Wyckoff nevertheless used the latest advanced technology and genetic testing machines available to successfully develop a profile. It was key to finding Jackie's killer: Only that person was likely to have the same DNA sequence.

Such profiles are entered into a special computer program containing an immense database of known genetic information for the U.S. population broken down by race to generate a "frequency statistic" that is used to demonstrate how common or how rare the sequence would be among the population.

That number might contain a dozen zeros or more. It could represent a number higher than all the people that have ever lived or died in the history of planet Earth. DNA profiles produce numbers in the millions, billions, trillions, quadrillions, even occasionally quintillions.

The sheet of paper containing the profile showed three rows of numbers, three single numbers, and thirteen sets of double numbers with graphs just above each; a complicated array to an outsider but as familiar as the dashboard of his car to Wyckoff.

There were sixteen loci, or locations, represented by sharp peaks in the graph and underlined with numbers representing specific scientifically known points on chromosomes. For each of the three single numbers there was a single peak. For each of the double numbers there were two peaks. Shown on the graph, the peaks resembled skinny stalagmites.

Each peak represented a particular site on a chromosome in a sperm cell. Wyckoff had spent years studying how to read these genetic signposts, and he knew that if the loci could be compared to another person, it would enable him to determine whether that particular person's DNA profile was "consistent with" the profile developed from the sample.

Wyckoff, ever the disciplined scientist, never uttered the word "match" when he appeared in court to testify about his findings. He never even used the word "match" in the lab.

He preferred the more accurate term "approximate frequency." If the profile revealed an "approximate frequency" of say, a billion, Wyckoff would testify that he would expect that a billion people would have to be tested before the same sets of numbers on the loci could be expected to again show up in the same precise order.

A defense lawyer would inevitably ask, "Is it possible?" that the number could belong to the DNA of a person other than his client. Wyckoff always answered yes. It was a possibility.

Just in time, Nash called again to say that he was in the parking lot. Wyckoff buzzed him in and took the envelope he had expected. There was no laughing or even small talk. Nash knew the lab protocol. Low-key. Always low-key. Anything said between the two of them could be the subject of cross-examination in a trial. The clerk signed a receipt for the evidence and Wyckoff took the evidence and went to work.

He had the lab to himself.

He put on a white smock and latex gloves. At a table covered with fresh butcher paper, he opened the larger envelope and removed the smaller envelope containing the samples of buccal swabs that had come from the mouth of Gerald Carnahan. He cut off one cotton tip and placed it in a tubelike device: a locking plastic vial about the size of the end of his little finger.

Then he sat at a special workstation that was decontaminated by ultraviolet light and bleach before and after each use to remove any residual DNA from previous analysis steps.

Heated water and a special detergent were added to the vial. This released DNA from the cell nuclei. He used a special pipette, which looked like an electric toothbrush, to transfer a minute quantity of the DNA-bearing clear liquid. He placed this in a plastic cartridge about the size of a tape player cassette that contained five narrow compartments, including one that held dozens of tiny black resin beads.

Wyckoff then placed the cartridge in a machine resembling a microwave oven. This was a Maxwell 16 "robot." It would take about eighteen minutes for it to purify the DNA, a process that consisted of further separating the DNA from other cellular components. The resin beads were key to this. The beads have a unique ability to change polarity, causing them to bind the DNA to cast off impurities, and then unbind the DNA into a pure solution. Unwanted proteins and salts were left behind.

While the Maxwell 16 hummed, Wyckoff prepared vials of reagents for the next step, involving a large thermal cycler, which targets cellular locations of interest through a special chemistry that allows minute quantities of DNA to be replicated to produce enough for a profile. After loading the sample into the thermal cycler, Wyckoff stepped outside the amplification room and locked the door. He drove home for a few hours' sleep and returned at 3 A.M. The process took three and a half hours.

When he returned, he was ready for the final step—profiling. The amplified DNA from the thermal cycler was placed in a genetic analyzer. It is a large machine, perhaps five feet tall, that separates DNA fragments as they pass through a glass tube. As the DNA fragments pass again and again through the tube, a laser causes them to fluoresce and that data is sent to an attached computer that makes the DNA fragments visible on a screen. It finally produced a single profile containing three rows of graphs and numbers.

In one hand, Wyckoff held the DNA profile developed earlier from the vaginal swab. This was the profile he managed to develop even though ReliaGene had failed four years earlier.

In his other hand, Wyckoff held the profile he had just produced, titled, "Standard From Gerald Carnahan."

Then he compared the numbers for the sixteen loci, the three sets of single numbers and thirteen double numbers each topped by one of the skinny stalagmites on the graph paper.

From the vaginal swab, he saw 14,18—6, 9.3—29, 32. 2—12—18—11, 12—10,11—10,13—9, 11—12, 13— 12—8,10—16,18—10, 13—8, 11—20,21.

From the sheet marked "Gerald Carnahan," he saw 14,18—6, 9.3—29, 32.2—12—18—11, 12—10,11— 10,13—9, 11—12, 13—12—8,10—16,18—10, 13—8, 11—20,21.

An outsider might have shouted, "It's a match!" But Wyckoff calmly carried the sheets to the population database computer and entered the numbers. In seconds it provided a readout:

"6,039,000,000,000,000,000."

This is 6.039 quadrillion. Meaning that before the

same genetic profile could be expected to turn up again, 6.039 quadrillion people would have to be tested.

Prosecutors privately call this kind of data a home run, a slam dunk, out of the park, a hole in one. But Wyckoff was not the type who high-fived or whooped. He never even drank coffee or ingested caffeine in any form. He was steady. Low-key. Professional. Always ready for the day when a defense lawyer would try to rip him apart on the witness stand.

Before Wyckoff could officially finish the case, his entire process would have to be reviewed by another qualified DNA analyst at the lab. Then he would issue a report that would state that the profile from Gerald Carnahan is "consistent" with the profile taken from the vaginal swab and had an "approximate frequency" of 6.039 quadrillion.

But even before his report would become official, a verbal notification from Wyckoff was sufficient under Missouri law to allow Nash to go to a judge and obtain an arrest warrant.

At 6:15 A.M., Wyckoff called Nash, who answered on the second ring.

In Springfield, Gerald Carnahan was unaware that he could measure his freedom in hours.

CHAPTER 29

--- ---------- ---

A TEAR IN HIS EYE—AGAIN

Sergeant Dan Nash had what he needed. He called his shift commander at the Highway Patrol headquarters in Springfield and asked for backup, then called a judge at home who agreed to sign an arrest warrant for Gerry Carnahan.

Investigator Mike Rogers of the Highway Patrol and a trooper were sent to Springfield Aluminum in Nixa to watch for Carnahan. If they spotted him, they were instructed not to let him out of their sight.

Nash called the Christian County Sheriff's Department. They agreed to send officers.

Workers showing up at the boat accessory plant passed unmarked police cars parked up and down the street. Rogers watched from the back of the parking lot.

With a warrant in hand, Nash pulled up at about 9 A.M. Carnahan had yet to show.

Finally, at just after 10 A.M., a minivan pulled up and parked in the spot marked "Reserved for Gerald Carnahan."

Carnahan got out of the van and started to walk toward the building but stopped. He saw Rogers and the trooper walking toward him. Nash was right behind them.

"Gerald, we have a warrant for your arrest for the murder of Jacquelin Sue Johns. Turn around and put your hands on your vehicle. Now," Rogers said.

Nash walked up as Carnahan was being patted down and handcuffed.

"This is the warrant, Gerry," Nash said. "We'll see that you get a copy."

As usual, Carnahan was well dressed. He wore a light sports jacket and pressed slacks. He looked like he might be on his way to a business meeting.

"You have the right to remain silent," Rogers told him. "Anything that you say can and will be used against you in a court of law. You have the right to an attorney. If you cannot afford an attorney, one will be provided for free. Do you understand your rights?"

Carnahan nodded. "Do you understand your rights?" Rogers repeated.

"Yes, yes I do," he finally said.

And then to his surprise, Nash again spotted a tear rolling down Carnahan's cheek, just as the day before when his mouth had been swabbed for DNA.

But except for the brief moment of tears, if Carnahan

was amazed at being arrested so soon after the DNA sample was taken, he didn't show it.

He was placed in the rear of a Highway Patrol cruiser. "Watch your head," Rogers said as Carnahan got into the backseat.

Moments later, the police grapevine went to work.

Sergeant Tom Martin got a call. So did Detective Rod Burk. Jackie Johns's father Les Johns was sitting in an armchair on his porch when the phone rang with the news. Minutes later, Les took the first of more than a dozen calls from newspaper and television reporters.

Jackie's sisters all quit what they were doing and headed over to their father's home.

Television stations cut in with the news—Gerry Carnahan was being processed at the Greene County Jail. The charges? The murder and rape of Jackie Johns.

Before long, it was all over the streets of Nixa and Springfield.

Former Christian County sheriff Dwight McNiel was home in Ozark sitting at his desk when he got a call from a Highway Patrol trooper who told him Sergeant Dan Nash had managed to get Gerry Carnahan arrested for the murder of Jackie Johns. McNiel was stunned.

When he found words, all he could say was, "Finally. I knew it would come. It had to come."

McNiel and his wife Marcella had just adopted a cocker spaniel puppy but hadn't picked out a name yet. The puppy lay on the floor, wriggling near his feet.

McNiel picked up the little dog and put it on his lap. The animal licked his hand and furiously wagged its tail.

"Your name is Nash," he told the dog. "Nash. That's a damn good name."

CHAPTER 30

THE PRAYER

Gerald Carnahan's arrest in August of 2007 for the 1985 murder of Jackie Johns began a grueling legal process that would peak when he finally faced a jury. It would attempt to provide answers to questions that had lingered for nearly a quarter of a century.

Would Jackie Johns's family—her father Les and sisters Jeanne, Joyce, and Janis finally see justice after twenty-two years? Would they be able to visit their mother Shirley's grave knowing that Jackie's killer had at last received what he had coming? Mother and daughter's tombstones lay side by side. Would Carnahan be sentenced to life in state prison? Or even sentenced to die in Missouri's execution chamber, with Jackie's family watching through one-way glass?

Or would Carnahan be freed to live out his life as a

wisecracking, middle-aged businessman with a tarnished reputation?

The law guaranteed that on the day Carnahan would face his jury they must presume him to be innocent.

But among the Johns family members, there had never been doubt about who killed Jackie. And now, according to what they had been told by prosecutors, irrefutable scientific evidence existed proving it was Gerry Carnahan and could not be anyone else on earth.

The old suspicion, rampant in the mid 1980s among tens of thousands of newspaper readers and devotees of the evening news in southwestern Missouri, that Carnahan was a killer, had finally resulted in an arrest warrant for murder.

And what a warrant! It stated that Carnahan's DNA profile matched the profile finally obtained from microscopic bits of semen found in Jackie's body to a certainty represented by a number with fifteen zeros. It meant that 6.039 quadrillion people would have to be profiled before the same series of genetic markers would be expected to again turn up in the same order. Who would even conceive of testing one quadrillion people? That's many times greater than the estimated number of humans who ever lived.

Les Johns was eighty years old and in frail health when Carnahan was charged with murder. Johns worried that he would die before the trial ended. He placed his hopes and prayers on that evidence, the so-called DNA match of 6.039 quadrillion to one. Quadrillion. Who would even think of challenging a number like that?

But Gerry Carnahan's father Garnett Carnahan did not have to go far to find a willing challenger.

Defense lawyer Dee Wampler had an office right in Springfield. He also had a reputation as the most tenacious defense attorney in southwestern Missouri, a title once bestowed on the previous Carnahan family attorney, Jack Yocom, who'd died four years earlier.

Wampler and his partner Joe Passanise would defend Gerry Carnahan.

Their opponents would be Darrell Moore, the elected Greene County prosecutor, and his young assistant Casey Clark.

But it was the styles of the lead attorneys, Wampler and Moore, that would most influence how the long-awaited murder trial took shape and would play out.

At first glance, both men appeared remarkably similar. Both were highly religious Christian family men. Both had served as chief prosecutor in the same Greene County prosecuting attorney's office. Both were Republicans.

But their differences foreshadowed a bitter court battle.

Wampler was a one-man publishing empire who had written five books, most with a religious and legal theme. He was about to publish a sixth, *One Nation Under God: A Trial Lawyer Exposes the Myth of the Separation Between Church and State.*

Celebrity gained from his career as an author led to dozens of appearances on television and radio talk shows.

During one such appearance before the murder trial,

Wampler revealed that he knew the secret of how to obtain the American Dream of happiness, family, and wealth.

His advice: Work hard, harder than anyone else. That was it.

"You don't have to be smarter than the next person," the seventy-year-old Wampler told the talk show's host. "You just have to work harder."

Wampler said his workday often began at 4 A.M. and ended at 10 P.M. And during all these work hours, his guiding star was the Christian Bible. He called it "our standard of truth."

And when it came right down to the common person fighting, say, a traffic ticket, Wampler was there, too. One of his four books on Missouri criminal law was titled *Defending Yourself Against Cops in Missouri and Other Strange Places.*

Among the scores of plaques and awards he had received were citations early on in his career for being selected "Springfield's Outstanding Young Man" and "Missouri's Outstanding Young Man."

Wampler's record of acquittals showed that when in a courtroom he shed any preacherlike persona in favor of a pit bull's demeanor. He was feared on cross-examination.

In contrast, lead prosecutor Darrell Moore did not exhibit a showman's demeanor. He was low-key in comparison. But he had won murder convictions in tough cases.

Moore had prosecuted a number of murder defendants, but Gerry Carnahan was unusual, not only because he was accused of having murdered an innocent young woman, but also because of his quirky personality. He displayed an unnerving familiarity with courtroom personnel, including Moore, which gave his staffers an uneasy feeling. For example, Carnahan kept on a first-name basis with Moore, whom he always called "Darrell." And when there had been a question of Carnahan's transportation from a court hearing in Clayton, Carnahan suggested that he should simply ride back to Greene County with Moore.

Both prosecution and defense realized that the looming legal fight would involve the DNA. But Moore knew he had been entrusted with what might prove an equally significant aspect of what was about to unfold. And that was the story of Jackie Johns herself.

He must never let the jury get so involved with numbers and science that they would forget that she had once been a loving daughter and sister. He had to find a way to "seat" her at the trial, and never let jurors forget that a woman of only twenty, on the threshold of life, had been thrown to the ground, raped, and beaten to death, then tossed into a lake and discarded.

At times, Moore quoted the Old Testament to colleagues.

"Murder is a stain upon the land. The blood of the innocent calling out for justice." They must have faith, he assured them. Justice would prevail. He would promise himself that when it came time for a final summation, he wouldn't let the jury forget Jackie.

As a prosecutor for ten years, Moore had dealt daily

with tragedy. But he had also dealt with tragedy on the most personal of terms. In 1987, he had held his two-day-old son, Alex, in his arms and cradled him until he died. Doctors told him they couldn't save the little boy's life. A rare condition involving the infant's intestines could not be treated in a way that would save the newborn. Nothing in Moore's life would ever be the same after Alex died.

"It was the hardest thing I've ever had to do," he said.

And yet, through this tragedy, Moore understood what victims' families went through and that they were still suffering even decades after a crime. During the most contentious part of the upcoming trial, Moore would find time to reassure Jackie's sisters. He would find them sitting on a bench in a courthouse hallway, dejected and grief stricken and worried that even with the DNA, Carnahan would again find a way to defeat justice.

Like all good prosecutors, Moore realized that DNA evidence alone, no matter what the odds of a profile match, would not add up to a guilty verdict in a murder case. There must be corroboration, some type of other evidence or witness testimony that can show a jury that a defendant committed murder. And the scientific results had to be explained so that a jury would believe them. But bring in witnesses who could put a defendant at or near the supposed murder scene and then properly present the DNA evidence, and Moore was confident that Carnahan would be convicted.

And yet, even with eyewitnesses there is always doubt.

Not that they are lying. The doubt comes in when they take the stand. Will they hold up? Most of them would be testifying about something that had occurred decades earlier. It was likely that they had forgotten much of it. Moore needed to find a way to get them ready to withstand a cross-examination by a relentless lawyer like Wampler.

———————

In the case of *State of Missouri vs. Gerald Leonard Carnahan*, the DNA evidence seemed irrefutable.

But Wampler and Moore both knew this wasn't true. The DNA actually presented a great opportunity for the defense to blow the case out of the water before it ever got near a trial date. After all, the vaginal swab from Jackie's autopsy contained only a minute amount of human material. Technicians at the Highway Patrol Crime Lab in Jefferson City couldn't find much of anything when the sample was sent to them in 1999. It had been examined microscopically but wasn't tested for DNA because no semen was found.

Four years later, ReliaGene in New Orleans, a highly regarded private firm, took a shot at testing the same sample. And while their technicians had discovered minute traces of semen, they found the sample too degraded to profile.

But just four years after that, however, the Highway Patrol Crime Lab came up with a monumental DNA profile, representing a number so large it sent people to online dictionaries for a definition of "quadrillion."

Still, Wampler said he doubted the sample, and he filed motions to exclude it from trial. He attacked it from a chain of evidence stance. How could it be found to be too degraded to test and then miraculously be tested again and a profile obtained? He knew that there were questions about where the sample had been stored. He knew of at least one police witness who would testify that when he had responsibility for keeping track of the vaginal swab he hadn't always known its whereabouts.

Wampler figured if his challenge to the admission of the swab worked and it was excluded from trial, the verdict could easily be not guilty. The witnesses who put Carnahan in his truck behind the 7-11, and even his brother Ken, whose deposition testimony put the truck near the spot where Jackie's car would be found, were vulnerable. Wampler just needed to work hard. Harder than Moore. Wampler relied on the power of work. Like he always said, it was the secret to the American Dream.

The DNA match was just another challenge for Wampler. It didn't matter if it was 6.039 quadrillion or 6.039 quintillion to one. He never doubted that he could overcome this evidence.

In August of 2007, soon after Carnahan's arrest, a bail hearing was held in Greene County Court.

Two deputies led Carnahan into the courtroom. He had the wild-eyed look of a trapped animal. Gone was the debonair demeanor of past years. It was impossible for him to appear suave, or even dignified, while wearing a baggy orange jumpsuit instead of his usual tailored sports jacket and slacks.

Since his last court appearance, at the attempted kidnapping trial fourteen years earlier, Carnahan had gained thirty pounds. His face now sagged. His hair was thinning. Instead of the faint smile that had puzzled and even angered some who'd attended his previous trials, his face was set now in a permanent frown.

At the brief hearing Carnahan whispered to Wampler and then stared intently at the judge. Wampler argued that his client had always appeared as required when released in the past, and should be allowed out on bail.

Prosecutor Moore opposed Carnahan's release under any conditions.

But the judge wasn't about to grant bail. After all, the Highway Patrol had found it necessary to ask U.S. Customs to inform them the moment Carnahan was spotted after exiting his plane at LaGuardia in New York City following a trip to Taiwan. Agents there watched him board a flight to Springfield and undercover state cops were waiting when he arrived.

Even if he gave up his passport, Carnahan might figure out some way to climb aboard a jet for Taiwan, a country with no extradition treaty with the United States, which would put him beyond the reach of any arrest warrant.

Bail was denied. Moore watched Carnahan's shoulders sag.

"His head just dropped," he told an assistant.

The Gerry Carnahan famous for getting out on bail during earlier scrapes would have no freedom. There would be no press conferences where he might again declare, "I'm just an average guy." A media entourage would not trail him. And his favorite newspaper reporter Ron Davis had moved on. Davis was now a television producer at KSPR in Springfield. He had assigned a reporter to the hearing.

Five months later, after Carnahan had received a psychological examination and was found fit, he was bound over to trial. A trial date was set for July of 2009.

Now, Moore and Wampler knew, was when the real pretrial legal infighting would begin.

However, during another pretrial hearing, both agreed to a strategic trade-off. Wampler allowed Moore to summarize in court papers much of the DNA information that would later be brought out during trial. And Moore agreed to give the defense early access to the prosecutor's evidence.

Despite what may occur on television court dramas, during a real murder trial (or, for that matter, any trial), there must be no surprises when it comes to what evidence is offered. Each side knows what the other side's witnesses will testify to, and what evidence it will present. This is the required "discovery" process.

Still, this does not guarantee no surprises will result when witnesses take the stand. No prosecutor or defense attorney can really know what will happen when a person is under cross-examination.

Gerry Carnahan was again taken to Greene County Court on March 6, 2008, and was again arraigned. The procedure was a mere formality. But the hearing included the first discussion about a change of venue. Carnahan was again on the front page and leading off the evening news. The familiar image of a smiling Jackie Johns, taken from a family portrait, was once again all over television. Even though Jackie had been murdered nearly twenty-three years earlier, the local publicity machine had resumed where it had left off, making it unlikely that an unbiased jury could be seated.

On May 28, 2008, Moore announced he would not seek the death penalty. This was a surprise. But the decision was a concession to Jackie's father Les Johns, who feared he would not live long enough to see Carnahan convicted if the death penalty was sought. Death penalty trials often take two or three years extra to prosecute.

Finally, on June 16, 2008, the case was transferred 250 miles to the east, to St. Louis County, where Judge Michael Jamison was assigned to preside. The courthouse was in Clayton, about nine miles from downtown St. Louis.

Jamison set an initial trial date of July 27, 2009, close to two years after Carnahan's arrest and twenty-four years after Jackie's death. Wampler and his trial assistant, attorney Joe Passanise, filed motions challenging the prosecution's DNA evidence from the Highway Patrol Crime Lab. The pretrial battling continued and the initial trial date passed. Another was set for February 16, 2010.

But there were distractions, including one that was unforeseen.

A phone call came in to Moore's office. It was Dee Wampler. He asked to stop by so they could talk.

When Wampler arrived, Darrell Moore knew something was terribly wrong. His adversary didn't show the confidence that usually made him the center of attention whenever he walked into a room.

Wampler's message was simple. He had kidney cancer and needed immediate surgery. The trial had to be delayed. For Moore, there was only one course of action. He would agree to a postponement. He didn't hesitate to tell Wampler.

The two men sat in silence for a moment.

Then Moore asked Wampler to join him in prayer. While the oath that Moore had taken as a lawyer compelled him to always fight for his client, in this case the people of Missouri, it didn't rule out prayer.

For maybe the first time in the state's history, two opponents in a murder case bowed their heads together and prayed for the same thing: that one of them would live to fight the other.

CHAPTER 31

TRIAL DAY ONE

By the time Gerald Carnahan's trial finally began on September 14, 2010, the St. Louis County Jail had been his home for nearly two years. It was a modern, state-of-the-art lockup designed to reduce violence through the use of nonthreatening building materials. It was bland and monotonous.

It was an unchanging, shadowless world painted light blue and white. There were no bars. Inmates were locked at night in individual rooms set along a kind of mezzanine. Below, in the day area where prisoners spent most of their time, plastic chairs and tables colored the same light blue gave the place the look of an elementary school classroom.

After the first two hundred days or so, Carnahan wrote to an acquaintance in Springfield that he felt like a goldfish constantly circling in the same, featureless aquarium, looking at the same seashell day after day.

But now the monotony was over. At least for the day. This was the first day of Carnahan's trial for first-degree murder and forcible rape.

Breakfast was the usual cereal, toast, coffee, and juice served on a foam tray. At 8 A.M. two guards took him to an area where he was allowed to dress for court. Carnahan changed into an outfit his family had brought over: a gray sports jacket, dress shirt, and tie. He pulled on expensive slacks. He exchanged his jail sneakers for dark leather shoes and black socks.

A guard led Carnahan to a secure waiting area. A half hour later two armed St. Louis County deputies showed up. They handcuffed him with his arms in front. Then each deputy held an arm and led him through a breezeway between the jail and the courts building in Clayton, a prosperous city and government center twenty minutes from downtown St. Louis. No words were spoken.

A short ride on an elevator closed to the public brought them to a hallway just a few steps from the prisoner entrance door to Division 23, the courtroom where St. Louis County Circuit Court judge Michael Jamison presided.

A deputy told him to sit.

Fifteen minutes later, another deputy unlocked the door and said, "OK. You're up."

His handcuffs were left on. The second deputy pulled the door open. The first person Carnahan saw was a uniformed armed bailiff who took his arm and led him to a chair at the defense table.

Gerry Carnahan's attorney Dee Wampler put his hand on his client's shoulder and smiled.

The bailiff removed the handcuffs and told him to sit. Two additional armed bailiffs watched from strategic positions between Carnahan and the packed seating area.

When Carnahan turned in his seat and faced the crowd, a change came over him. He was again the center of attention, said some of those who attended his trial. The moment had arrived after years of waiting. Wampler had told him the case looked good for the defense. DNA or no DNA, there was still plenty of doubt, his lawyer had said. Wampler had told him that the case was so old there would be plenty of opportunities to challenge witnesses. Twenty-five years had passed. There were dozens of questions about the DNA evidence that had been stored in unrefrigerated boxes.

In the crowd, Carnahan immediately spotted his second wife, a woman from mainland China, sitting with his father. They had two daughters, aged six and eight, but the girls did not attend the trial. His stepmother Barbara sat in another row farther back. He spotted his brother Ken, who would not meet his gaze. The prosecution had subpoenaed Ken. As a witness, he would have to leave the courtroom once the jury was brought in.

Jackie Johns's sisters Jeanne, Janis, and Joyce sat together on the side of the courtroom opposite where Garnett Carnahan and his wife sat. The rows closest to the front were filled with mostly younger men and women, presumably media.

He didn't see former sheriff Dwight McNiel. Or Tom Martin of the Highway Patrol. Both would be testifying later, so they weren't allowed inside the courtroom. Carnahan glanced over at the prosecution table. He recognized Darrell Moore. Beside Moore sat young assistant prosecutor Casey Clark, who looked like a boyish Clark Kent.

Wampler handed Carnahan a yellow legal pad and a soft-tipped pen. Wampler's assistant Joe Passanise, who sat at the end of the table, smiled.

"All rise," shouted the bailiff. "This court is now in session. The Honorable Michael Jamison presiding."

Jamison wasted little time. Assured that both sides were ready to begin, he said, "Bring in the jury." All in the courtroom stood until the jurors had filed in.

"Please be seated," Jamison said. He nodded to the prosecution table. "Mr. Moore? Are you ready with an opening statement?"

"Yes, Your Honor," Moore said. Clipboard in hand, he positioned himself in front of the jury.

Moore spoke of a "road map" that would make it clear that Jackie Johns, a young woman with no connection to Carnahan, had been kidnapped, raped, and beaten to death with a heavy bumper jack. He laid out the chronology so familiar to the victim's family members and the police who had worked for years to solve the case.

Moore said there would be stops along the road map where witnesses, including the defendant's brother, would place Carnahan's 1961 Chevrolet Apache pickup truck at the very place where Jackie was last seen and near where her blood-spattered Camaro would be found the next morning. Moore made it clear that police had interviewed Carnahan and he had denied ever having any kind of social or romantic relationship with Jackie. In fact, the only time he ever saw her was when he stopped at the Sale Barn Café to eat, or during the few months that Jackie had worked on the production line of the Carnahan family boat accessory business in Nixa.

There would be grisly autopsy photos, Moore warned jurors. They had to see them, he explained. They had to understand exactly how Jackie died.

And they had to understand Jackie herself. This was a promise he had made to the Johns family. The promise stemmed from the humanity that had deepened within him when he had held his newborn Alex for the little time the infant boy was alive.

They had to understand Jackie. They had to know who she was. He had to show them that she was worth caring about. He would make them never forget her.

After twenty minutes, Moore brought up the DNA.

This would be the clincher, the irrefutable link to Jackie's killer, he said. And that killer would not only have a name—Gerald Carnahan—but a number. And that number was 6.039 quadrillion to one. He told the jury the odds of the DNA belonging to anyone but Carnahan were so incomprehensible that the lab wizard who had cracked the DNA profile, Jason Wyckoff, would have to explain it.

When it was Wampler's turn, Carnahan started taking notes.

He knew that his attorney, who believed so strongly in the power of hard work, was his key to acquittal.

But Wampler was slow out of the gate. He relied on time-tested defense clichés. He reminded jurors that the defense did not have to make an opening statement. He said, "A coin has two sides." He asked them not to hold it against his client if he didn't take the witness stand. Silence was Carnahan's right under the Constitution, he said.

Wampler said his heart poured out for Jackie's family. That she was an innocent and beautiful woman who had been widely liked. But then he bore down on the heart of his case. There was doubt. There was "more than enough" for reasonable doubt, he said. And if there was reasonable doubt then they would have to find Gerry Carnahan innocent and let him return to his life in Nixa.

Wampler told jurors he would present evidence that would show that of at least twenty-eight people who drove down Highway 160 on June 17, 1985, the night Jackie was last seen at the 7-11, not one of them remembered seeing his client's pickup. None remembered it, even though it was a classic Chevy from the 1960s with a bad muffler.

He said the chain of evidence connected to the vaginal swab taken from Jackie's body at autopsy was so flawed that one high-ranking Springfield Police Department officer had written a report stating, "I can't tell what's what."

But Moore leaped to his feet with an objection at that. The officer who wrote the report was deceased. He could not be cross-examined. His report would be hearsay and thus not allowed to be heard by the jury.

Jamison summoned both attorneys to his bench. Out of earshot of the jury, they held a "sidebar" conference.

Then the judge said, "Step back." Wampler resumed his opening statement but never again mentioned the deceased officer's report.

Instead, he hit hard on what prosecution witness Gene Gietzen, the former director of the Springfield Police Department forensic lab, was expected to say on the stand. And that would be that of the 189 separate items painstakingly pulled from Jackie's Camaro and labeled, including human hairs, none could be connected to Carnahan.

A partial fingerprint taken from the interior overhead lightbulb, the light where the dome lens was missing and was never found, did not match his client, Wampler said. It came from someone other than Carnahan or Jackie. All of the hairs were excluded as having come from Carnahan. None of the blood matched his.

And as for the DNA itself, he asked, who could trust any conclusion obtained from that sample? He told the jury that they would hear testimony that the sample had been degraded beyond use because it had not been consistently refrigerated. Property logs that were supposed to keep track of this evidence at all times were missing from the Springfield Police Department, he said.

Finally, Wampler told them that the witnesses who

claimed to have seen Carnahan's truck behind the 7-11 about the time when Jackie had gone inside to buy her cigarettes and hair spray had changed their stories. They now remembered more than they did twenty-five years earlier. And one in particular, Wampler said, his voice rising, was an admitted liar who claimed to have seen Carnahan that night parked at the 7-11 just to get even with him because of a feud over an outboard motor. Wampler told the jurors that this witness, Allyn Wollard, would admit that he lied again and again to the grand jury about his own former drug use. That he denied using drugs, but when pressured under oath and threatened with prison, admitted not only to having used them but to having sold marijuana.

"Herbert Allyn Wollard is a liar," he said.

When Wampler finished and sat down, observers said they saw Carnahan smile. They said he looked relaxed. Like the old Carnahan. The one who couldn't be caught.

CHAPTER 32

REASONABLE DOUBT

Defense attorney Joe Passanise stood before the jury. He turned to his left. Herbert Allyn "Al" Wollard faced him from the witness stand. It was the morning of Day Two of the trial, September 15, 2010. Wollard was the first witness. He had already testified about having spotted Carnahan's pickup behind the 7-11.

Wollard's testimony was crucial. It would put Carnahan and his noisy old Chevy truck behind the 7-11 at about the same time Jackie was last seen coming and going at the store. DNA might be the glamour evidence. But corroboration, putting the defendant in a position where he had opportunity to commit the crime, was just as important.

But now it was cross-examination time for the defense.

Passanise held a yellow pad on which he had written

"Lies" and then "Number 1, Number 2, Number 3" and so on through "Lie Number 7."

The jury could not read the lawyer's pad. And he didn't really need the notes. They were just a precaution. He was so familiar with the pages and pages of police reports, grand jury testimony, and depositions that the moment Wollard lied, if he would lie on the stand, Passanise would know. And then he would pursue the lie until Wollard revealed himself as a witness who could not be believed.

Wollard's testimony was as critical to Carnahan's fate as an alibi. Wollard had been Carnahan's buddy for a decade until they had a falling-out over an outboard motor and a union strike at the Carnahan family's factory, Springfield Aluminum. The strike was two months before Jackie died in June of 1985. Wollard was thirty-three at the time.

Wollard testified that he placed the anonymous call to Crime Stoppers a few days after Jackie's body was found to say that he'd seen Carnahan's truck parked behind the 7-11. It was this anonymous call, which cops easily traced to Wollard, that first fingered Carnahan. And what better witness could be found than a former buddy who had known Carnahan for years? Who had hung out with him? Drank beer with him, played volleyball with him? Al Wollard was a perfect Judas, except for one thing: He was a liar. And jurors didn't have to take just anyone's word on that. Not when Wollard openly admitted it on the witness stand.

"Lie Number 1: You told officers you weren't involved with drugs," Passanise said.

"That was a big fat lie," Wollard testified.

Passanise paused. He gave jurors time to think for a few moments about what Wollard had just said.

And then he asked a series of questions about Wollard's drug use. As for marijuana, according to quick calculations of daily use over years that Passanise made on the spot, Wollard admitted to having smoked it about six hundred times. Wollard also testified that he would go on cocaine binges for days.

Lie Number 2: When police interviewed him a second time in 1985, Wollard denied ever dealing drugs. But on the witness stand, with Carnahan staring intently at him, Wollard said yes, at one time many years earlier he could have been considered to be a drug dealer. In answer to another question, Wollard tallied the drinks he'd had on that Monday as a "couple of beers" at one bar, two more at home, and maybe three more during a trip to a second bar.

Passanise reminded Wollard that, according to a police report, he told Sheriff McNiel and Detective Rodney Burk that he had been drinking on June 17, 1985, the night Jackie was last seen and the same night that Wollard said Carnahan's truck was behind the 7-11. But on the stand at the murder trial he first answered that he hadn't been drinking, but then, when pressed by Passanise, corrected himself.

"Which is it?" asked Passanise.

"I was drinking that night," Wollard said.

Passanise turned to the jury and said, "Lie Number 3."

He then asked, "Have you ever given incorrect information under oath?"

Wollard answered "No."

An incredulous Passanise looked at the jury, then asked, "Are you sure?"

Wollard answered "Yes." Lie Number 4.

The cross-examination wore on for an hour as Passanise checked off each "Lie" listed on his sheet. Wollard remained calm, even when Passanise repeatedly said, "Is that a lie?"

Lie Number 5, 6, and 7 could have been attributed to a failing memory, especially since twenty-five years had passed since that night Wollard claimed to have spotted Carnahan's truck. He was asked if he had really yelled "Fuck you" to Carnahan during the strike at Springfield Aluminum. In statements to police at the time, Wollard said he just kind of yelled and gave him a "Bronx cheer."

He'd also told police that later that same night he met Joyce Johns, Jackie's sister, at a bar. He said they talked for more than an hour. But employment records proved that Joyce Johns had been at her job that night.

And, during a volleyball game at a mutual friend's house several days after Jackie's body was found, Wollard told police he did not speak to Carnahan. But under cross-examination on the witness stand he said he had spoken to him, but there had not been hard feelings over the strike or the outboard motor. Wollard admitted under questioning that he might have said at times that he would like to see Carnahan "rot in jail," and probably did predict that his former buddy would "get his own," meaning punishment.

And finally, Wollard testified that he wasn't sure of the date of the night that he saw Carnahan's truck behind the 7-11, but he was certain it was the night Jackie was last seen.

Moore, the lead prosecutor, handled the redirect questioning that followed. Wollard said he wasn't sure of the date, but he was sure of the day of the week that he saw the truck. And because it was a Monday and a work-day, he said, he would not have been using drugs. He testified that while he had been drinking that night, he hadn't used any drugs. As for lying to police, to a grand jury, and to the prosecutor's office in Christian County, he said he had lied to protect himself.

"Everything else is the truth," he said now on the murder trial witness stand. "I know what I saw and I saw the truck."

Passanise got still another shot at Wollard.

"You lied to everyone until this year. The prosecutor had no idea that you lied. Why should we believe you now?" he asked.

"Because I'm telling the truth," Wollard said.

Passanise asked Wollard if he should be prosecuted for perjury.

Prosecutor Moore objected, stating that the statute of limitations had expired.

Jamison, the judge, sustained the objection.

Passanise pressed on. He focused on Wollard's statement to police just a few days after Jackie's murder, that he had talked to Joyce Johns at a bar, a statement that couldn't be true, police had determined.

"You re-clarified because law enforcement spent time investigating what you told them and found out it wasn't true. That's why you took it back," he said.

"I was mistaken," Wollard said. Those were his last words that morning on the witness stand.

At 11:35 A.M. Jamison called a recess for lunch. Wollard was told to remain in the courthouse to be available to the defense should they call him as a witness.

Dee Wampler gathered up some files and strode past where Jackie's sisters stood together. He looked pleased. His man Passanise had done what he had been assigned to do: bring out the lies in Wollard's story. He knew the jurors must be asking themselves, did this guy, a buddy turned enemy, really see that Chevy pickup on that night?

Darrell Moore could see that Jackie's sisters were distraught. He knew that murder trials had their high points and their low points. Wollard had done about as well as could be expected. But when a witness under oath admits telling a "big fat lie" to the police, it never sits well with a jury.

He reassured the sisters that the trial was far from over. The most damning evidence against Carnahan, the DNA, was yet to come. There would be two witnesses for that, one from ReliaGene in New Orleans and the Highway Patrol's own technician Jason Wyckoff. It was irrefutable, he said. And both witnesses were steady under questioning.

But the sisters could not be consoled. After all this time, and after Wollard's startling testimony, it seemed to them like Carnahan would somehow manage to wriggle free. Their father Les was at home in Nixa, too ill to attend the trial hundreds of miles away. His daughters had reserved rooms at Clayton hotels, planning to stay for the duration of the trial.

Back home, a television reporter interviewed Les that day. Speaking very slowly, and pausing to catch his breath, he said he hoped and prayed justice would be done. But he said he had considerable doubts that Carnahan would be convicted. Too many years had passed. There were too many questions about the DNA.

Moore huddled with his assistant, Casey Clark, a young prosecutor. Moore had a key role planned for Clark.

Clark was soon to be married. His wedding day was just a few days away. But first, he had an important assignment: He was to handle the direct examination of a key witness, Gina Pineda, the ReliaGene lab DNA testing supervisor who would be asked about the state of the vaginal swab she unsuccessfully tried to test in 2003. The defense would no doubt try to get her to say it was so degraded it could never be reliably tested. And while that was true in 2003, Clark would have to skillfully and carefully bring out her testimony that new techniques in genetic profiling made available in 2007, when Gerry Carnahan was arrested for the murder, could indeed result in a DNA profile even from as little as a few semen cells.

At 1:13 P.M. the trial resumed. Wade Pearce raised his right hand and swore to tell the truth. Pearce, who'd once rode motorcycles with Carnahan and also drove an older model pickup truck, was shown photos of the area around the 7-11 from that Monday night in June of 1985. Pearce said that when he turned to drive behind the 7-11 to return to his home in a trailer park nearby, he saw Carnahan's 1961 Chevy pickup parked behind the convenience store in such a way that it would have allowed him to spot customers stopping in the parking lot in the front. But he said he didn't remember seeing anyone in the truck.

Under questioning, Pearce told the jurors that he appreciated vintage trucks and had one himself, a 1956 GMC with a long bed. He testified that he and Carnahan were friends and had ridden motorcycles together years earlier. He said Carnahan once came into the grocery store where Pearce worked and offered to buy his 1956 GMC pickup. But Pearce said he had declined the offer.

He testified that police showed him a "lay down" of six color photos of similar-looking pickup trucks. He had picked "C" as the truck he saw behind the 7-11. "C" was identified as Carnahan's truck.

But that had been a quarter of a century earlier.

It was Wampler himself, the lead defense attorney, who cross-examined Pearce. Wampler had copies of the statements Pearce had given Springfield detective Rod Burk twenty-five years earlier.

Pearce admitted that at the time in 1985 he told investigators that he had seen the truck for only "a split second." He admitted he said then that he wasn't sure what he saw. He had not been able to remember if the truck he saw had spoked wheels. Carnahan's truck had spoked wheels.

"Is your memory better now or was it better then?" Wampler asked.

"Better then," Pearce said.

Wampler brought out that at the time Pearce had said he couldn't say for sure that it was Carnahan's truck.

"I know what I saw, Dee," Pearce said.

"Didn't you say then, 'I can't say for sure because it was dark'?"

"I know what I saw," Pearce said again.

Wampler told Pearce that he should have realized that investigators were goading him into saying he saw Carnahan's truck.

At that, Moore stood and said, "Objection."

"Sustained," said Jamison.

Wampler turned to the desk reserved for the defense. Carnahan had written something on a notepad and wanted his lawyer to read it. Wampler glanced at it and nodded.

Finally, Wampler showed Pearce a document that stated that twenty-five years ago, just days after he claimed to have seen Carnahan's truck, Pearce had told Burk and McNiel that he didn't remember if the truck had backed into the area behind the 7-11, or if it was pulled in cab first. And yet in answer to an earlier question from Wampler, Pearce said it was backed in.

"Hasn't your testimony today been reckless as to your answers given to this jury?" Wampler asked.

"I saw what I saw," Pearce said again.

"Nicely programmed to say, 'I saw what I saw,'" Wampler said, before sitting down.

Carnahan's brother Kenny was the next witness. At 2:44 P.M. he raised his right hand and swore to tell the truth. Onlookers later said Carnahan stopped taking notes and crossed his arms, eyes on his brother. He leaned back in his chair.

In 1985, according to a transcript of his statement, Ken Carnahan told then sheriff Dwight McNiel and testified at several grand jury sessions that he had seen his brother's pickup truck on the CC side road just off Highway 160 near the 7-11. This was after he had returned with his father's Cadillac from a country humor show in Branson. His father and stepmother rode back with other family members. Ken Carnahan said he was given the task of driving the Cadillac back from Branson. He testified he dropped the Cadillac off at his parents' home just a half mile or so from the trailer owned by Jackie's parents where she also lived. He then picked up his own truck and his wife and children. They were with him when he claimed to have seen his brother's truck.

Ken Carnahan put this at about 11:15 P.M. to about 11:45 P.M. on the night of June 17, 1985; around the time Jackie was last seen. It was an old story. In the years that had passed, Ken had remained at the family's business. Moore stood before him and asked some of the very same questions that Dwight McNiel had asked years before. But this time Ken Carnahan's answer was, "I don't recall." He repeated it again and again.

Shown copies of his statement to Dwight and of his testimony before the Christian County grand jury, he didn't argue. "If that's what it says, then that's what it says."

Ken Carnahan told Moore that when he spotted what he guessed was his brother's truck, he saw only the rear of it on a foggy night from a distance of seventy-five to one hundred yards. Shown a copy of his statement to McNiel that it was more like fifty yards, he said again, "If that's what it says."

When asked if his distance judgment was better in 1985, he said, "It's better now."

Under persistent questioning by Moore, Ken Carnahan said that he only vaguely recalled his brother telling him that if he was called before the grand jury not to say that he had seen his truck parked that night on CC.

Shown a statement he had given to McNiel that not only had Carnahan told him to say that, but also that Ken had become angry when he had heard it, he answered, "I just don't recall."

Under cross-examination by Wampler, Ken said that in the days after Jackie's body was found he had "felt like a yo-yo on a string," being pulled all ways by police, the prosecutor Tim McCormick, and during several appearances before the grand jury.

"They had us so confused we didn't know what was what," he said on the witness stand.

He testified that he and his wife had considered moving away to get away from police who he said were harassing him by knocking on his door late at night.

He insisted that in 1985 he told investigators that while the truck he saw looked like his brother's, he could not be sure that it was. When he left the stand forty-five minutes later, he was in tears. When he later passed Moore in a hallway during a recess, he said, "Thanks for treating me with respect."

Tom Martin, who retired from the Highway Patrol as a lieutenant, was the final witness on the second day. He testified to what had been found in Jackie's bloody Camaro. He told of retrieving Jackie's body from the lake. He told about being called away from the investigation of Jackie Johns to work a double homicide in Taney County involving the bludgeoning death of a twenty-nine-year-old woman and her nine-year-old son. That case was still unsolved, he said.

CHAPTER 33

DWIGHT'S DAY

When he heard a bailiff call his name, former Christian Country sheriff Dwight McNiel stood and stretched. He had been waiting in the hallway outside the courtroom where Carnahan was on trial. He would be the morning's first witness.

When McNiel took the stand, jurors saw a self-assured fifty-seven-year-old private investigator in a business suit, who also happened to be chairman of the Missouri Board of Private Investigator and Private Fire Investigator Examiners. If any remnant existed of the old Dwight, the one who had bailed out of the sheriff's department long ago, frustrated by his inability to nail Gerry Carnahan for the murder of Jackie Johns, it didn't show. The one-room walk-up, where he lived after he left the sheriff's department, was just a memory. His highly successful private investigation agency, Midwest Intelligence, Inc., of Ozark, had replaced McNiel & Associates, the agency he once ran out of his apartment, the agency that had no associates. And after twenty-five years, there was frosting on the cake: Carnahan was finally facing a jury that could send him to a prison cell for life and McNiel was there to help that along.

During the trial, Judge Jamison had ordered his bailiffs to keep witnesses outside the courtroom, so McNiel had instead spent hours sitting in the hallway. His wife, Marcella, a trained paralegal adept at shorthand, took meticulous notes but avoided talking about or showing them to her husband. She was taking the notes so that Les Johns, who stayed in Nixa because he was too ill to attend the trial, could follow the proceedings in detail. McNiel would not be allowed to read the notes until the testimony of witnesses had concluded.

When McNiel noticed Carnahan sitting smugly at the defense table, wearing a suit far more expensive than his own, McNiel felt the old animosity. Carnahan hadn't given Jackie a chance. He had thrown her away like trash. While he had spent a few years in prison, Carnahan had gotten away with killing Jackie for years, and had enjoyed a quarter of a century of living off the wealth of his family. He had flown numerous times to Taiwan on extended business trips. He always flew first class. As McNiel would later recount, he steadied himself mentally as he made his way to the witness stand; it was time to make Carnahan ante up for all the grief he had caused.

For three hours, McNiel told of his involvement in the case, first to lead prosecutor Darrell Moore and then during cross-examination to lead defense attorney Dee Wampler.

Wampler worked hard to trip him up. It was his trademark, to work harder than the next guy. But the questions were too familiar. McNiel had spent weeks going over depositions and reports from the original investigation. And he knew that if he wasn't sure or did not remember, to simply say so.

It was well into the lunch hour when he was excused and left the stand.

Garnett Carnahan passed him in the hall. But the men did not speak. Jackie's sisters looked away. McNiel noted that they looked anything but hopeful. He couldn't blame them. Gerry Carnahan was a cat with nine lives.

McNiel knew that Gene Gietzen, who had headed the regional crime lab in Springfield, would be the next witness. Gietzen, a friend, had since retired and ran his own forensic consulting business.

McNiel was confident his friend would back up his own testimony. He had testified many times. He, too, knew to stick to what he remembered. He knew Gietzen's testimony would be crucial because it would set the foundation for the DNA evidence. It could give the defense room to try to convince the jury that it could not be trusted. The vaginal swab had not always been refrigerated. It had sat on a shelf for years in a room without air-conditioning at the Springfield Police Department. But McNiel wasn't worried. DNA had been found in Egyptian mummies and profiled. It had been found and charted in the frozen remains of 30,000-year-old mammoths. Cable television broadcasted shows about this kind of techno-wizardry all the time.

At 1:16 P.M. Gene Gietzen was sworn in and took the stand. Moore again handled the direct questioning. The first thirty minutes went smoothly. The highlight occurred when Moore handed him three Polaroid photos, one by one, and asked Gietzen to identify what they showed. He held each up and studied it.

They depicted sperm cells as viewed through a high-powered microscope, he said.

The photographs were of sperm samples taken from Jackie Johns during autopsy.

Another photograph showed head hairs taken from Jackie. Under a microscope, they were fractured, Gietzen testified.

"It takes great force," he said, "but hairs can be broken when struck by a metal object."

He said the object could well have been a bumper jack.

There was little for the jury to doubt. Microscopes were no more mysterious than test tubes. And at least some of the jurors were old enough to remember Polaroids. Hairs that break? Moore had hoped that women on the jury might link that to split ends. It sounded very plausible.

Wampler handled the cross-examination. He asked about hairs that had been found in the Camaro. Gietzen said he wasn't sure how many had been found. But he agreed that many hairs had been collected from the car's interior that were determined under microscopic analysis to not have come from Jackie or Carnahan.

There were arm hairs and pubic hairs, Gietzen said. But not one of them was matched to hairs collected from Carnahan. None of the fingerprints matched Carnahan, and none of the blood was linked to him, Gietzen said.

Earlier, during direct examination, Gietzen had testified at length about blood spatter. He was expert in its analysis. Most of it was found in the driver's-side rear seat area. But there was minute blood spatter throughout the car.

His answers painted a detailed picture of what must have been a horrific struggle that had gone on in the cramped interior of the Camaro. It would seem that if Carnahan were indeed the attacker, if he had pummeled Jackie with his fists, then at least one of his hairs would have been left in the car. Or a drop of his blood. Wampler asked Gietzen why, if Carnahan was the killer, none of his client's body hairs, tissue, or blood had been found in the Camaro. Gietzen answered that he did not know why.

Then came questions during cross-examination about the chain of custody. Had the samples from the autopsy always been held in the custody of police? Gietzen had testified that he did not know precisely how and where the Jackie Johns evidence had been kept after he left the police lab in 1990.

After a weekend break when there was no testimony, Gina Pineda of ReliaGene in New Orleans took the stand the following Monday. Moore was concerned that if her testimony was undermined, it might spread doubt about his star witness, Highway Patrol DNA technician Jason Wyckoff, who would testify after Pineda. The job of handling the direct examination of Pineda went to his top assistant, Casey Clark.

Clark patiently took Pineda through the history of the vaginal swab after it had been received at the lab in New Orleans. She freely admitted that semen cells were detected only through the use of a powerful microscope. And she said that even though a DNA profile had appeared tantalizingly close in 2003 when she supervised the testing, there had not been enough seminal material to obtain a DNA profile.

Pineda testified that she had reviewed Wyckoff's testing procedure and found it unflawed.

She did not waver on cross-examination. When Wampler pressed her on how such a minute amount of material could be profiled—less than a billionth of a gram—she answered that even smaller amounts had resulted in profiles used in successful prosecutions.

Next on the stand was Jason Wyckoff. Dressed in a conservative blue suit, Wyckoff, the man who would not drink coffee because the caffeine might affect his ability in the lab, patiently described the DNA testing procedure at the State Highway Patrol Crime Lab.

He testified that his title was "criminalist" and that he had appeared as a court witness forty times for the prosecution but only one time for the defense. He carefully explained that in general if genetic material is degraded to the point that it cannot be tested, it will not give a false profile. Only one profile was possible, he said. If a sample were degraded past testing, no profile would result.

Under cross-examination, Wyckoff answered that as far as he knew none of the items had been refrigerated in the Jackie Johns murder case. He admitted that "excessive heat" could be a factor leading to degradation of a sample.

He said the vaginal swab from Jackie's autopsy was the oldest material he had tested in a court case.

Wyckoff never once raised his voice. He answered each question easily, or stated that he didn't know. After less than two hours in the stand, Wyckoff was excused. He hadn't even broken a sweat.

Fifteen minutes later Moore stood and told Judge Jamison, "The state rests."

CHAPTER 34

- - - - - - - - - -

SARA TAKES THE STAND

The first defense witness called in *State of Missouri vs. Gerald Leonard Carnahan* was his former stepdaughter Sara Collins. The defense began their case on Monday, September 20, 2010. She was also his only witness. The defense would rest their case early the next morning.

The now forty-four-year-old woman, who had been a friend to Jackie Johns, stared straight ahead as she walked through the crowded courtroom to the witness stand. All the spectator seats were full. Newspaper stories about her anticipated testimony had assured there would be standing room only in the courtroom. Her mother, Pat Collins, Carnahan's ex-wife, sat near the back of the courtroom.

In 1985, when Jackie Johns died, Sara Collins was a nineteen-year-old college student who wanted to become a dentist. On the day of her testimony, her hair was dyed black and she wore dark clothing. To some of the onlookers, she looked "Goth-like." To others it appeared she was in mourning.

Collins was Carnahan's alibi. She was his best chance for an acquittal. He looked intently at his former stepdaughter. But she kept her gaze on defense attorney Dee Wampler, who began his direct examination.

And then jurors heard Collins preface her answers with an unusual phrase. It was unlike anything normally heard in a court of law from a witness.

To many of Wampler's questions, Collins first said, "According to the transcript," and then finished her answer. But she held no transcript in her hand. Wampler held no transcript. There was no transcript anywhere in sight.

Judge Jamison did not intervene.

Darrell Moore, the lead prosecutor, did not object.

Some of those who watched, those who knew Collins and had heard her talk of how badly she had been treated when she was interrogated during the days after the murder, speculated about the strange wording.

Her tone was flat, almost hostile. Was it because she didn't remember what really happened? Had she blocked it out? Or was it a way of protecting herself from the painful memory of events that had obviously changed her life, maybe for the worse? Or was she simply bitter at being caught up in the whole unsettling trial?

Wampler guided Collins through the basic elements of her story concerning where her stepfather had been on the night Jackie was last seen. She had told it before a grand jury and to police so often that she testified she couldn't remember how many times specifically it had been.

"When did you get home from work?" Wampler asked.

"According to the transcript, I worked eight to five," Collins said.

Marcella, Dwight McNiel's wife, was in the courtroom taking notes on Les Johns's behalf. She wrote the abbreviation "ATT" at the beginning of most of Collins's answers.

Sara Collins's story was basically unchanged except for one crucial detail. When she first spoke with police, she'd said that she and her former stepfather had gone to the Repair Shop in Springfield, a bar that served food, where Carnahan had a few beers and she drank soda because she was too young to drink alcohol. And then she drove him home around 8:30 P.M.

Collins then left to go buy a curling iron but could not find one she liked, so she had returned to the family home in Springfield on South National Road at around 9:30 to 10 P.M. She said she found Carnahan at home and believed he had never left.

The detail that would change was that on the witness stand she testified that she later claimed to have learned that Carnahan had also left on an errand, a trip to buy beer and visit the Vara Warehouse where two friends were building shelves for the business. But she insisted he was back home by the time she returned from shopping for a curling iron and never left again that night.

This was crucial from the prosecution's viewpoint, because it marked the only significant change in her story from what she originally told police. It was a possible wedge, a way to convince jurors that maybe she wasn't so sure that Carnahan hadn't had time to sneak out and murder Jackie. When Tim McCormick, the Christian County prosecutor in the 1980s, first heard about it, he had mocked Collins when she appeared before the grand jury.

"And just when did this occur to you?" he had asked sarcastically.

But Sara Collins remained adamant during her testimony at the murder trial that she had returned at about 10 P.M., in time to watch Johnny Carson's opening monologue with her stepfather. The Carson show began at 10 P.M. Carnahan was there, she testified, and never left until both went to work together at Springfield Aluminum the next morning.

Under questioning from defense attorney Wampler, Collins said that one day shortly after Jackie's body had been found, two security guards and Detective Rod Burk met her at her college campus in Springfield and told her she had to accompany them to the Springfield Police Department. Collins said she didn't want to go but finally agreed to follow them in her own car to the police department.

Once there, Collins testified that Burk verbally abused her and, when she tried to leave, grabbed her arm and told her she was not free to go.

"Don't touch me," she testified she'd told Burk.

Burk had accused her of having an affair with her step-father, Collins said, adding that she had vehemently denied the accusation because it wasn't true.

"It was terrible," she told Wampler. "There was no truth to it."

On the morning after Jackie disappeared, Collins testified that she drove Carnahan to work in her Dodge Colt because his truck was not running properly. In fact, his old truck had been parked for part of the day on Monday, June 17, 1985, on Highway 160, not far from where Jackie's Camaro would be found the next morning.

Collins told the jury that on that morning, she and Carnahan noticed the Camaro surrounded by police cars and officers, as they drove to their jobs. She denied being under Carnahan's influence then or on the day she testi-fied in the murder trial. And she continued to preface many of her questions by saying, "According to the tran-script."

She testified she was certain that after she came home from looking for a curling iron, Carnahan never left the house again that night. That would mean that at around 10 P.M., when the witnesses said they saw Carnahan behind the 7-11, he was home with his stepdaughter. And she testified that because Carnahan's truck had a bad muffler she would have been awakened if he had started it up to leave.

She was a light sleeper, she said. She would have heard the truck cross over cattle guards in the road that were near the house. Cattle guards, or metal tubing embed-ded in pavement that a hoofed animal will not step on, are designed to keep cattle off certain busy roadways. However, when a vehicle passes over the guards, the tubing makes a loud rattling sound.

And finally, Collins talked about being stalked by Jackie's mother, Shirley Johns, who had died in 1988. Collins said Shirley would routinely follow her, sometimes shouting "bitch" from her vehicle. She said that once, as she was standing at the mailbox in front of the house on South National Road in Springfield, Shirley "came over the hill" at a high rate of speed, causing Collins to jump out of the way. However, no charges or police report were filed.

Moore, the lead prosecutor, handled the cross-examination. He asked only a few questions. He asked about why she changed her initial story that Carnahan hadn't left the house after both returned from the Repair Shop. Collins said she simply learned afterward that Carnahan had gone to the Vara Warehouse, but didn't initially realize it that night. It was something they hadn't talked about, she said. But she answered that while she considered it unlikely, it was possible that Carnahan could have left the house that night without her knowing.

Wampler asked a few final questions. Was she sure Carnahan was there the whole night?

"He was there when I went to sleep and there when I woke up," Collins said.

If he had started the noisy old Chevy truck and had driven across the cattle guards, she said, "I think I would have heard it."

CHAPTER 35

LAST WORDS

Television prosecutors always manage to wrap up a trial closing argument in about twenty seconds. They unerringly come up with stirring moral arguments. And they never say "uh."

Law school students know that a closing argument must be concise and should connect all the evidence. And when a closing is very good, the jury is left with some noble conclusion to ponder back in the deliberations room.

But reporters who cover courts know that in most trials, final arguments, both for the prosecution and the defense, do not inspire. There is too much ground to cover. Even if a memorable line gets delivered during the hours of summarizing, jurors are often too mentally worn out to appreciate it. Or to even notice.

It was prosecutor Casey Clark's task to lay out to the

jury what the prosecution had to legally prove in order to convict Gerry Carnahan of murder and rape. This was the first and easiest part of the prosecution's closing argument. His boss Darrell Moore would do the rest.

Clark had to show that Jackie's murder had occurred sometime between 10:30 P.M. on June 17 and 5 A.M. on June 18, 1985; that she had been forcibly raped; and that she'd died as the result of blunt force trauma. He also had the responsibility of showing jurors that Carnahan had deliberately killed Jackie and had not simply accidentally struck her in the head during a struggle.

It took him more than an hour. When he got to the deliberation requirement, he pointed out that Dr. Dix, who had performed the autopsy, determined that Jackie had been struck four times with the bumper jack. Dix found fractured hairs, which illustrated the force of the blows.

"There was deliberation in his pausing between strikes," Clark said.

Clark knew that defense lawyer Joe Passanise, who would be the next to speak, would slam Al Wollard, the witness who said he saw Carnahan's pickup behind the 7-11 but also admitted on the stand that he had been lying about his drug use of many years before.

But Wollard's testimony was backed up by Wade Pearce, Clark said, who also told police that he saw what he thought was Carnahan's truck behind the 7-11. And Pearce had no secret drug use in his history.

"Compare them to Sara Collins," Clark said. "None of her statements can be backed up by other evidence."

When it was his turn, Passanise went right to the heart of the defense argument. He asked the jurors to put "emotion and sympathy" aside and to focus on what he called how witnesses' testimony had changed over twenty-five years. And this could only mean, he said, that they were either lying or were unsure of what they'd seen or heard.

Passanise reminded jurors that Pearce had initially told investigators he didn't know if Carnahan's truck was backed in or had pulled in front first. But during the trial he said it was backed in. Passanise asked how Pearce could remember something more precisely after so many years.

And Wollard's testimony should not be taken seriously, Passanise said.

"He does not know the meaning of truth. He was caught in his lies."

But the big show was Wampler versus Moore. And Moore, as prosecutor, would have the last word.

Wampler zeroed in on the vaginal swab that seemed to irrevocably pin his client to the murder.

"The traveling vaginal swab," he called it, noting that this evidence spent four days in Lake Springfield until Jackie's remains were found. He mocked how the swab had been kept in an evidence room with no air-conditioning. He asked the jurors if they really had confidence that the police knew at all times where the swab had been. It had been sent in 1999 to the Highway Patrol Crime Lab and in 2003 to a testing firm in New Orleans.

Then he shifted to hairs and fingerprints.

Wampler pointed out to the jurors that none of the hairs or prints matched Gerry Carnahan. And some pubic hairs found in her panties did not match her or Carnahan.

"That's probably the murderer there," he said.

He recalled that Carnahan, when he voluntarily came in to be questioned a few days after Jackie's remains were found, had invited Sheriff McNiel and Detective Burk to search his truck, and he later invited them to come out to his house and look all around.

"Look at [my] clothing, truck, drain, soil samples, trash, go ahead," Wampler said loudly, paraphrasing his client. "Is that what a murderer is going to do?"

And finally he came to the DNA sample. "Take a pink diet sugar," he said. "That's one gram . . . A nanogram is one billionth of that package. And that's what they tested."

Moore opened with a time-tested prosecutor's approach.

"The defense is like a squid," he said. "They started shooting out ink to sidetrack you."

Then he began a methodical running down of the evidence.

"The swab remained in the chain of custody," he said. "This evidence was always there."

He called Sara Collins the "star alibi" for Gerry Carnahan but reminded jurors that she had answered that it *was* possible her stepfather could have left the house that night without her noticing.

" 'If he left, I didn't know.' That's what she told you," Moore said.

As for the DNA evidence, he asked, "Where did the sperm come from? It came from him. The answer is what the science told us. He was the source. He was out that night. He opened the trunk, got the jack, and hit her four times. He meant to kill."

Referring to the day in August of 2007 when Sergeant Dan Nash of the Highway Patrol and his team confronted Carnahan and swabbed the inside of his mouth for buccal cells to be tested for DNA, Moore said, "He had a tear in his eye. He knew after twenty-five years, science and justice had caught up with him."

The thought that justice would finally prevail, that's what Darrell Moore fervently hoped would ring in the jurors' ears.

CHAPTER 36

- - - ——————— - - -

VERDICT . . .

Jackie Johns's sisters stood as the jurors filed out of the courtroom. The final arguments were over and the judge had read the jury instructions. The evidentiary part of the trial had finished.

Jeanne, Janis, and Joyce had attended all six days during the first-degree murder and rape trial of Gerald Carnahan—the man they were certain murdered their youngest sister Jackie twenty-five years earlier.

Bailiffs led Carnahan, wearing a neatly pressed gray suit, through a side door to a secure waiting room for defendants who had not been released on bail.

After waiting a quarter of a century to see Gerry Carnahan face a jury for the death of their sister, the waiting for a verdict was about to begin. It was shortly after noon on September 22, 2010, a Wednesday.

Their eighty-three-year-old father Les Johns waited at

home in Nixa, too ill to leave the house. He had predicted for years that he would not live long enough to see Carnahan face justice. Now, a verdict might come within hours.

Dwight and Marcella McNiel waited side by side on a bench in the carpeted hallway.

Dayna, who had been Jackie's close friend and confidante and now worked for McNiel's private detective agency, had remained in Nixa. She had printed Marcella's daily accounts of the trial and then brought them to Les Johns.

Darrell Moore sat near the McNiels.

His assistant Casey Clark left and went to his future in-laws' home in St. Louis. He was going to be married on Saturday. He called Moore every few hours as he ran wedding errands with his soon-to-be wife.

Down the hall, defense attorney Dee Wampler paced.

Gerry Carnahan's Chinese wife waited outside the courthouse with his brother Ken and father Garnett. Wampler promised to call them when a verdict came in.

Reporters lounged on the floor, typing stories on laptop computers to send to their editors. Ron Davis, the former *Springfield News-Leader* reporter, was one of those editors, now working for a Springfield television station as a senior producer.

As the hours passed, tempers wore thin.

No messages were sent from the jury to Judge Jamison asking for portions of testimony to be reread or to answer a legal question. Their silence was unnerving. At many trials, jurors often send notes to the judge asking for clarification or direction.

Wampler looked at his watch. It was 7 P.M.

"Dwight, they have been out for seven hours. Know what that means? That's real good for the defense," Wampler said.

He slapped Dwight McNiel on the back.

"Eff you, Dee," McNiel said. "You are full of it."

The Johns sisters looked pleased by McNiel's remark. But there was still an uncomfortable distance between the former sheriff and the Johns family. They had been angry for so long over his failure to arrest Carnahan for Jackie's murder, even though plenty of other investigators had also failed.

At 8 P.M., Judge Jamison summoned everyone back to the courtroom. The jurors were sent home for the day. They would start again on Thursday morning at 9 A.M. Jamison warned them not to discuss the case with anyone or to read, watch, or listen to any news accounts of the trial.

Moore watched the Johns sisters. He could see their anger. When they got outside, Jeanne headed for her own hotel. Joyce and Janis walked toward another hotel's parking garage.

Moore would later recount the close call he had convincing the sisters to remain at the trial.

When Moore caught up to them, they told him they weren't staying. The waiting was too much. They were tired. Their nerves were frayed. They were sure the jury would return with a "not guilty" verdict. They couldn't bear to watch Gerry Carnahan stroll out of the courtroom. But Moore persisted.

"He's going to be found guilty," Moore told the sisters. "You've got to stick with this. It's not over. He's not getting off. You have to have faith."

But they wouldn't listen.

Moore followed them to the elevator that took them to the parking garage.

They said again and again that they were fed up and were going back to Nixa.

The elevator door opened just as Moore's cell phone chirped. It was a text message from Dean Dankelson, the Jasper County chief prosecutor.

"Tell the family I am praying for them," the text read.

Moore put his hand out and held the elevator door open and showed the text message to the Johns sisters. He held his cell phone out for them to read.

"You are not alone in this," Moore told them. "Everyone you know is praying he will be found guilty. He's not going to escape."

Joyce and Janis looked at Moore. Tears rolled down their cheeks.

"I need you. Please say that you will stay," Moore said. "Tomorrow. You will see tomorrow that I'm right. He's not going to get away. I know it."

The sisters looked at each other and hugged. They would stick it out. There was something so sincere about Moore's belief that Carnahan would finally get what was coming to him that it allayed their fears. They called their sister Jeanne, who also agreed to come back the next day and wait for a verdict.

At 9 A.M. on Thursday, the three sisters waited together.

Six more hours dragged by.

Finally, a clerk walked quickly through the hallway to the courtroom just before 3 P.M.

"There's a verdict," she said.

Dee Wampler hurried into the courtroom, followed by Darrell Moore.

McNiel stood and began to walk toward the courtroom door. Then he stopped and turned to his wife.

"Here it comes, Marce. I have a really good feeling. I pray it's going to be what it needs to be," he said.

They found a seat in the front, not fifteen feet from where Carnahan sat. The sisters sat together at the other end of the wood bench in the first row of the gallery. Across the courtroom, Carnahan's wife sat with her father-in-law Garnett Carnahan and his wife. Ken Carnahan returned to the courtroom and sat beside his father.

Newspaper and television reporters claimed their seats. Each sat in a part of the courtroom where they could see Carnahan's face and document his expression when the verdict was read.

At his future in-laws' home, Casey Clark sat on a couch beside his fiancée. Their wedding was little over a day away, and they were all getting ready for the rehearsal. Minutes earlier, Moore had called Clark and told him the verdict was in and promised to call as soon as he could to let him know what it was.

The sisters waited in silence.

Garnett Carnahan stared straight ahead. His son's wife was in tears.

It had been a long time since Jackie died. Her sisters thought of their mother and how she had grieved the loss of her youngest child. Her grief had killed her, they believed. Could they even dare to hope for a guilty verdict after all this time?

"All rise," the bailiff said as Judge Jamison strode to his seat. The bailiff told everyone to remain standing for the jury.

The jury filed in. Jamison told all to be seated.

"Have you reached a verdict?" Jamison asked the jury.

Deborah K. McLaughlin stood and said she was the foreperson. "Yes, Your Honor, we have," she answered.

"Please pass the verdict forms to the clerk."

The clerk passed the forms to Jamison, who reviewed them and then gave them back to the clerk who returned them to McLaughlin. The courtroom became unnaturally quiet.

"Please read your verdict," the judge said.

In a clear voice, McLaughlin read, "On the count of murder in the first-degree in the death of Jacquelin Sue Johns, we find the defendant, Gerald Leonard Carnahan—guilty."

A collective "yes" came from the Johns sisters. They collapsed onto one another crying.

McLaughlin continued reading the verdict on the rape count.

But the word "guilty" could barely be heard over the cheers.

Dwight McNiel squeezed Marcella's hand and told her, "It's done."

He would later tell Marcella that he didn't see any reaction or emotion in Gerry Carnahan's face to the first guilty verdict. When the second guilty was spoken, he still didn't flinch.

"I wonder if he even understands what just happened," McNiel said.

Gerry Carnahan's wife began to cry. Garnett Carnahan and other family members rushed to console her.

Judge Jamison struck his gavel.

————————

Back in Nixa, Les Johns waited. He had never let go of his quest to get justice for Jackie. He had mourned his daughter and then his wife. Throughout the twenty-five-year ordeal, he'd kept the memory of his murdered daughter alive. He persisted, granting newspaper interviews to mark the anniversary of Jackie's death. He refused to allow what had happened to his youngest child to be forgotten. He had never let anyone doubt the killer was Gerald Carnahan. "I will never forget," he often told reporters.

The call to Les came within five minutes of the verdict.

"It's hard to believe that it took twenty-five years to get us here," he said during the interviews that followed from his Nixa home. Then he dropped his guard and smiled.

But it wasn't over.

———————

Back in the courtroom in Clayton, testimony on sentencing was about to begin.

Prosecutor Darrell Moore read from Gerry Carnahan's rap sheets. Jurors were told about his convictions for attempting to kidnap Heather Starkey from a Springfield street, and how he'd broken into and tried to burn down the aluminum foundry in Aurora. Jurors heard about the Geo Tracker he'd pushed down a hill because he felt like it. They heard how he fired a shotgun into the floor of his home and then kicked police officers who showed up to arrest him.

McNiel watched the jurors as they heard all about Carnahan's past for the first time, a grim history that residents of Nixa and Springfield had known for years.

When they heard about the other crimes, McNiel thought the jurors seemed astonished. He said some sat back and shook their heads. Others, he said, stared intently at Carnahan, as if truly seeing him for the first time.

What couldn't be told because of the rules of evidence was how Carnahan remained a prime suspect in Debbie Sue Lewis's murder. Debbie Sue hadn't been mentioned during the trial or in the original arrest warrant at all. But she wasn't forgotten. News stories about Carnahan's arrest for murder in the Jackie Johns case mentioned her, and Carnahan was still the only publically identified suspect in her case. Her father Elmer Lewis stayed glued to the television set back in Springfield whenever a story about Carnahan was shown. His wife Marie, Debbie Sue's mother, had died.

Nor was it mentioned anytime in court how some investigators persisted in a belief that Carnahan had also murdered Kelle Workman. Or that Carnahan was also still suspected of involvement in the baffling disappearance of the three missing women from Springfield: Sherrill Levitt, her daughter Suzanne Streeter, and Suzy's friend Stacy McCall, though the media also revived the loose links to Carnahan despite police never having officially questioned him about the case. No evidence had ever turned up to suggest what had happened to them.

At the conclusion of the sentencing hearing, the jurors returned to the deliberations room to decide a punishment for Carnahan. The minimum sentence could be as little as five years. They returned after an hour.

The jurors recommended the maximum: life in prison without the possibility of parole for the murder, life in prison for the rape.

Dwight and Marcella McNiel watched as Carnahan heard the sentencing recommendation and then leaned over to Wampler.

McNiel said he heard Carnahan lean over and ask his attorney, "When do I get out?"

On the drive back to Ozark, Dwight McNiel turned his cell phone off. It had been ringing constantly. Tom Martin called after hearing about the verdict. McNiel's son, an account executive, called and offered his congratulations. Several private investigators from around the state called, too.

Of course, Dwight McNiel would never say that he finally nailed Gerry Carnahan. He never claimed that. In the end, it was Sergeant Dan Nash of the Missouri State Highway Patrol who set in motion the events that led to the DNA match and Carnahan's eventual conviction. McNiel had tried the best he could, but in the end no man had caught Carnahan. Rather it was a scientific process that finally made him pay. And it was the hundreds of interviews and preservation of the physical evidence that were crucial to sealing Carnahan's fate. DNA alone would not have been enough.

McNiel never doubted that Carnahan was Jackie Johns's killer. Even when it looked like there was no way that Carnahan would ever pay for it, he never wavered. Whenever he was asked, McNiel would tell fellow investigators that he was certain Gerry Carnahan had murdered the pretty waitress from Nixa.

"It's time to leave it all here," McNiel told his wife as they drove west on Interstate 44 through the edge of the Ozarks. "Let's just leave it alone."

But even as he spoke the words, he knew he could not make good on that promise. Letting go just wasn't in his nature. Carnahan had not been charged with any other murders, but McNiel felt certain there were more victims.

"He's killed other women. I'm sure of that," McNiel said as he sat in the office of his home on the banks of the Finley River in Ozark six months after Carnahan began his life sentence.

McNiel was thinking of Debbie Sue Lewis and Kelle Workman. Sherill Levitt, Suzie Streeter, and Stacy McCall were still missing. Maybe in another few years a scientific advancement could break those cases, too. It was possible.

He would keep coming at Gerry Carnahan. He would contact him in prison. He would insist on an interview. McNiel said he would rely on Carnahan's love of attention, his guilty conscience, and the fact that he had nothing to lose. It could lead to a break in the unsolved cases. He just had to wait until the right time.

"He'll talk to me eventually. I've got no doubt about that," McNiel said.

"It's something that I am absolutely sure about. I can't tell you exactly why. I just know that he will. And when he does, he'll tell me all that he's done. He's a serial killer. He's got a lot to talk about."

EPILOGUE

- - - ─────── - - -

On October 25, 2010, Gerald Carnahan was formally sentenced. He appeared before Judge Jamison who, at least in theory, had the power to give him a sentence that would allow him to someday be free.

But the jury had recommended life without parole for the murder and life for the rape of Jackie Johns. And that's what he got.

Carnahan appeared dressed in a tan prison-issue jumpsuit. His hands were cuffed in front.

When asked to make a statement, he spoke briefly but never mentioned Jackie.

He never said the words "I'm sorry." His final words before the sentence was pronounced were about himself, and placed the blame elsewhere.

"I had ineffective assistance of counsel from my lawyer during my trial," he said.

Afterward, his chief trial lawyer Dee Wampler said that by saying that he was ineffective, his client was simply preserving a motion for appeal.

It wasn't unusual, Wampler said.

Les Johns had planned to make it to the sentencing where he could for the first time stand face-to-face with the man who had raped and killed his daughter, but his illness prevented that from happening.

Instead, his daughter Jeanne made a statement from the witness stand.

She tried valiantly to get through what she had written but broke down at the end.

Later, she told a reporter she wanted the judge and the entire world to know that by murdering her sister, Carnahan "did more harm than he could ever know."

"There's never closure," she said. "But he is paying for his crime and he'll never be able to do it again."

When the verdict came after the end of testimony in the murder trial in September, Wampler was interviewed by a number of reporters.

"It was going our way right up to the science," he said, referring to the DNA match. "We couldn't put our client on the witness because of his record. And that hurt us."

The day after he was sentenced, Carnahan stood for a mug shot at the Eastern Reception, Diagnostic and Correctional Center in Bonne Terre. His prison number is 505305.

He was listed as five feet nine inches and 258 pounds, nearly 100 pounds more than on that day long before when Dwight McNiel first laid eyes on him at the political fund-raiser. It was the day in September of 1984 when Gerry Carnahan, wearing the Louis Vuitton scarf, showed up with his new wife, Pat Collins.

That was the year Jackie Johns won the Nixa Sucker Day beauty queen contest.

In May of 2011, Gerry was moved to the tough, ultra-maximum security Potosi Correctional Center, where Missouri executes its condemned prisoners.

The Nixa Sucker Day festival was held on May 13 and 14 of 2011. The second day, Saturday, was cold and rainy. Despite the weather, a couple of thousand festivalgoers crowded the five-block downtown.

On the street, Jackie's sisters, Janis, Joyce, and Jeanne, manned a booth under a sign "Jackie Johns Memorial Scholarship Fund." Each year for twenty-five years the fund has awarded a scholarship to a deserving Nixa High School senior. In July of 2011, the local rock band the UnMistaken held a concert for the scholarship fund at the Shrine Mosque in Springfield. The event was standing room only.

Jackie's friends Dayna Spencer, the former police officer, and Lisa Fitzpatrick Shaw, a wife and mother, met at the festival to catch up. Dayna worked the booth with the surviving Johns sisters.

Dan Nash, who still works for the Missouri State Highway Patrol, stopped by to say hello to the women in the booth. He continues to climb mountains and lead expeditions.

At the junior high school at one end of the block area, the Sucker Day beauty contest was held.

The competition featured toddlers, preschool, and school-aged boys and girls, singing and dancing in a mini-production on the stage in the school's gymnasium. Family and friends waved at the kids during their acts.

The judges included two women from a show in nearby Branson called "Maids of the Titanic." They sat at the judges' table in full costume and wearing their stage makeup.

The winners still receive rhinestone tiaras and sashes.